PTE ACADEMIC PREPARATION BOOK

PEARSON TEST OF ENGLISH

PRACTICE EXAMS

IN SPEAKING, WRITING,

READING, AND LISTENING

WITH FREE MP3s, SAMPLE ESSAYS,

AND ANSWERS

PTE Academic Preparation Book: Pearson Test of English Practice Exams in Speaking, Writing, Reading, and Listening with Free mp3s, Sample Essays, and Answers

© COPYRIGHT 2020 Exam SAM Study Aids & Media dba www.examsam.com

ISBN: 978-1-949282-39-9

NOTE: PTE Academic and Pearson Test of English are trademarks of Pearson, Inc. This publication is not affiliated with or endorsed by Pearson, Inc.

TABLE OF CONTENTS

PTE Academic Test Format

The practice tests in this publication simulate the format and level of difficulty of questions on the real Pearson Test of English, also known as the PTE.

The PTE consists of the following sections:

Part 1 – This part of the exam consists of the speaking and writing sections.

Speaking Test:

The speaking tests contains 35 items in total, and the questions are of the following types:

- Read paragraphs aloud – 6 items
- Repeat sentences – 10 items
- Describe graphs, charts, or other images – 6 items
- Listen to brief lectures and provide oral summaries of each one – 3 items
- Listen to brief questions and provide answers – 10 items

Writing Test:

Summary writing and argumentative essay writing skills are needed for the writing section of the exam. This section consists of four items:

- Read texts and write summaries of them – 2 items
- Write argumentative essays from prompts – 2 items

Part 2 – Reading Test

The reading test consists of 15 items. You will need to select multiple responses for some of the items. This part of the exam has the following types of questions:

- Read a passage and select single answer from multiple-choices – 2 items
- Read a passage and select multiple answers from multiple-choices – 2 items
- Review jumbled paragraphs and place them in the correct order – 2 items
- Read texts with gaps and fill in the blanks from a list of words provided – 4 items
- Read texts and fill in the blanks from multiple-choices for each gap – 5 items

Part 3 – Listening Test

The listening section consists of 17 items. You will see the following types of questions on this section of the exam:

- Write summaries of each recording – 2 items
- Choose multiple answers for question on each recording – 2 items
- Listen to recordings and fill in the missing words in the gaps in the texts – 2 items
- Choose the correct summary of each recording – 2 items
- Choose single answer for question on each recording – 2 items
- Choose words that are missing from the end of a recording – 2 items
- Listen to recording and indicate incorrect words in the texts provided – 2 items
- Listen to sentences and write each one exactly as it was spoken – 3 items

How to Use This Book

There are three practice tests in this publication. In practice test 1, we have provided tips and examples before the speaking and writing sections to help students gain strategies on how to answer the various types of questions on these parts of the PTE. We suggest doing practice test 1 in untimed conditions to become acquainted with the testing strategies, and then completing the other tests while timed.

Computer Access

The response times provided on the accompanying mp3s assume that the student has computer access. In order to simulate the written input on the speaking and listening parts of the test, you should open the sound files in one window on your computer, and enter your responses into a word-processing system in another window of your computer.

Note to Educators

Please remember that this book is copyright. If you are going to use this material with a class, you are not allowed to copy the material in any way. If you need multiple books, please contact us via our website as we offer substantial discounts for multiple purchases.

Personal Introduction

In this introductory part of the test, you will briefly give some information about yourself. You will have 25 seconds to read the question and prepare your response. You will then be given 30 seconds to speak. This item is not scored.

Strategies for Reading Aloud

Bear in mind these factors as you respond to the reading aloud items on the speaking test:

- Reading Speed – For these types of questions, you will need to be sure that you speak at a good pace, so you should spend no more than 35 or 40 seconds reading each text.
- Pronunciation – Pronounce each word as correctly and as clearly as you can. You score will be affected if poor pronunciation would cause the listener confusion about your meaning.
- Emphasis – You will need to read the text with the correct emphasis. You should place strong primary emphasis on the most important concepts, and secondary emphasis on the concepts with somewhat lesser importance. Note that nouns and adjectives typically receive emphasis over other words when reading a text aloud.

Read Aloud Practice

Now select the recording entitled "Reading Aloud – Example" at:

pte-listening.examsam.com

1) Listen to the recording and notice how the nouns and adjectives are emphasized when reading aloud.
2) Then listen again and pause after each sentence, trying to repeat it with the same emphasis as the speaker.
3) Finally, listen a third time while looking at the example and suggested answer on the next page.

Read Aloud – Example

Various systems of chemical notation have been created over the past few centuries in order to record important chemical compounds through a shortened series of characters or symbols. In addition, computerized systems that display complex chemical interactions are now commonplace in the scientific community.

Suggested Answer

The words with primary emphasis are <u>underlined</u>, and the words with secondary emphasis are in *italics*.

<u>Various</u> systems of <u>chemical</u> <u>notation</u> have been created over the past few centuries in order to record <u>important</u> <u>chemical</u> *compounds* through a <u>shortened</u> <u>series</u> of *characters* or *symbols*. In <u>addition</u>, <u>computerized</u> *systems* that display <u>complex</u> *chemical* *interactions* are now <u>commonplace</u> in the *scientific community*.

Repeat the Sentence Questions – Tips

These types of questions assess your pronunciation, emphasis, and speed, as well as your comprehension.

As you attempt practice test 1, listen to each sentence and repeat it multiple times to check your speed, emphasis, and pronunciation.

Note that the texts for all of the speaking questions are included in the answer key at the end of the book.

Describe the Image – Tips and Useful Phrases

For six of the tasks of the speaking test, you will have to describe information on a chart or graph and draw conclusions about it. Here are some tips for this part of the test:

1. As a general rule of thumb, you can think of this task as having two basic parts:
    a) Introducing the data – You will need to say what is being represented.
    b) Reporting on significant details – You will need to talk about high points, low points, and aspects that remained the same.

2. The following words and phrases are useful when describing images:
    *   The graph (or chart / illustration / image / map) shows (or displays / exhibits / highlights / indicates / presents / represents / reveals) . . .
    *   The smallest / greatest difference . . .

4

- The largest / smallest increase (or decrease) . . .
- At its highest / lowest . . .
- This is followed by . . .
- The second-largest was . . .
- It has declined / gone down / decreased (or risen / gone up / increased) constantly / dramatically / gradually / significantly / slightly / substantially / steadily.
- It dipped (or diminished) slightly / modestly.
- The most noticeable aspect . . .
- One can discern that . . .
- It remained stable / constant / the same / unchanged.
- It was equally balanced.
- It has fluctuated / risen / fallen / reached a peak.
- We can conclude that . . .
- We can draw the conclusion that . . .

Describe the Image – Example:

Now look at the graph below and review the example response on the next page.

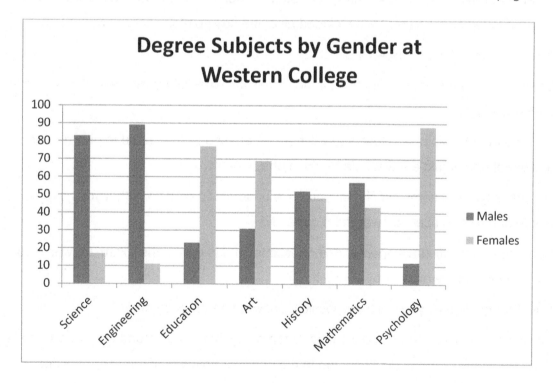

Describe the Image – Sample Response:

The graph represents enrollment in seven subjects for men and women at Western College. The greatest gender difference is in engineering, with an 89% male enrolment, compared to only 11% women. This is followed by science, which showed an enrolment of 18% women, but a much larger cohort of 82% men. Psychology, education, and art are largely female-dominated areas, while mathematics had 57% males and 43% females. Finally, history was more or less equally-balanced in terms of gender.

Re-tell Lecture Questions – Tips

For these types of questions, you will hear talks or lectures. After listening to each one, you will have 10 seconds to review your notes. Then you will be given 40 seconds for each one to restate its contents.

You need to be sure to include all of the key points from each lecture, so you should take notes as you listen.

Listen to each lecture in Practice Test 1, and practice taking notes on each one.

When you have finished, compare your notes to each of the suggested answers in the answer key to be sure you have included all of the key points.

Answer Short Questions – Tips

Students encounter many situations in academic life where they will have to respond to brief questions.

In this part of the speaking test, you will hear 10 questions. You need to give a brief answer of one or just a few words for each one.

So, these types of items check that you have understood questions that you have been asked and that you can answer them correctly.

Sometimes you will have open-ended questions on this part of the exam, for which you have to think of the answer by yourself.

For other questions, you will hear possible answers on the recording.

To respond to these types of questions, listen carefully to understand which words have been emphasized in the question and to the possible answers, if they are provided.

PTE Speaking Practice Test 1

The lecture texts, correct answers, and suggested responses for all of the items are included in the answer key at the end of the book.

Now open the recording entitled "Speaking Practice Test 1" at:

pte-listening.examsam.com

Follow the instructions on the recording as you attempt the practice test that follows.

Read Aloud

For items 1 to 6, read the text aloud as clearly and as naturally as you can, at a good pace, and with good pronunciation and emphasis.

Item 1:

A computer system is called a "turnkey system" when it is purchased from a supplier as an assembled unit in which the necessary software is already installed within the required hardware. Businesses that prefer turnkey systems do so because there is usually no need to perform any system analysis or design exercises on computers acquired in this way.

Item 2:

The term "business cycle" refers to the tendency for profit-making activity within any country to fluctuate over time, rather than experiencing steady growth. Such fluctuations have existed ever since economic record-keeping began and can be caused by factors such as natural catastrophes, changes in banking policies, and political upheavals, including revolution and war.

Item 3:

The World Health Organization was established in 1948 within the United Nations in order to promote international cooperation in global health issues. The control of diseases is its primary concern, but it also assists in vaccinations, water supply, and sanitation around the world. In addition, it is in possession of a great deal of information relating to drug abuse, nuclear hazards, and cancer research.

Item 4:

Located in South America, Brazil is a low-lying land mass within the Amazon basin on the east side of the continent, where the forest canopy was cleared in order to create timber reserves. It was settled in the sixteenth century by Portugal and has an almost entirely tropical climate, with average cumulative annual rainfalls of up to 80 inches.

Item 5:

The turn-over tax is charged during the production process, as goods are transformed from raw materials to finished products. For example, bakeries pay it on flour, carpenters pay it on wood, and sometimes the customer will even pay it on the final product. Unlike other taxes, no credit is offered against the tax for amounts previously paid.

Item 6:

The Canadian water weed is a plant that is native to North America. It can grow up to nearly four meters in height and has white flowers with dark green leaves. Many years ago, the weed was introduced to Europe, where they are now sometimes regarded as a nuisance because they frequently block waterways.

Repeat the Sentence Questions with Tips

For items 7 to 16, repeat each sentence exactly as it is recorded. You will hear each sentence only once.

Describe the Image

For items 17 to 22, describe each illustration in detail. You are allowed 25 seconds to study each illustration, and then you will need to speak for 40 seconds on each one to give your response.

Item 17:

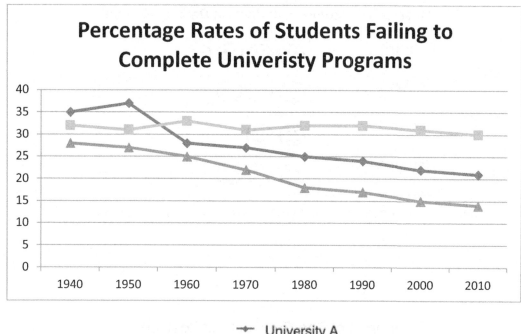

Percentage Rates of Students Failing to Complete Univeristy Programs

- University A
- University B
- University C

Item 18:

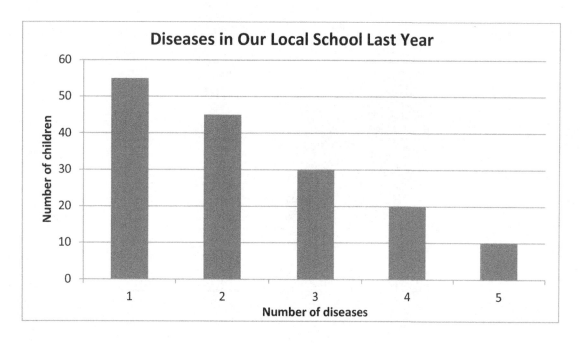

Diseases in Our Local School Last Year

Item 19:

This Quarter's Customer Satisfaction Data by Region

Region 1	😊 😊 😊 😊
Region 2	😊 😊 😊
Region 3	😊 😊
Region 4	😊 😊 😊

Each 😊 represents positive feedback from 1,000 customers.

Item 20:

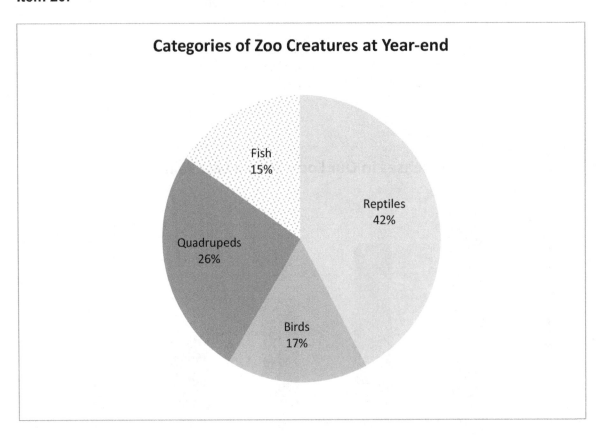

Categories of Zoo Creatures at Year-end

Fish 15%
Reptiles 42%
Quadrupeds 26%
Birds 17%

Item 21:

Data on Monthly Accidents in Springfield

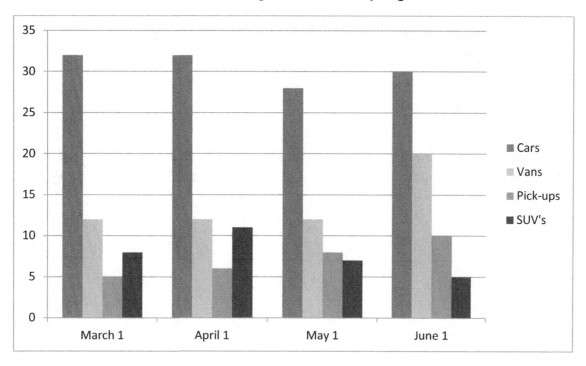

Item 22:

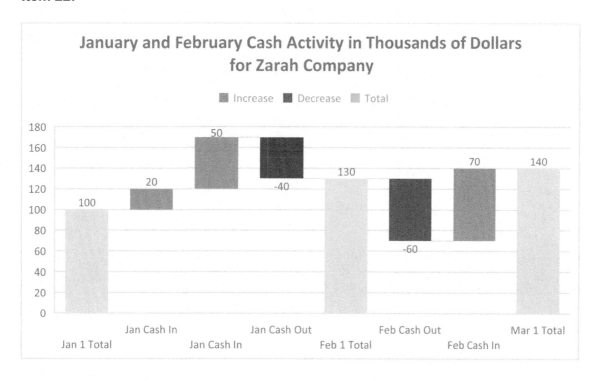

Re-tell Lecture Questions

For items 23 to 25, you will hear talks or lectures. After listening to each one, you will have 10 seconds to review your notes. Then you will be given 40 seconds for each one to restate its contents.

Answer Short Questions

For items 26 to 35, you will hear 10 questions. You need to give a brief answer of one or just a few words for each one. For these questions, you should speak immediately after the beep.

Improving Your PTE Writing Skills with Essay Samples

PTE Writing Task 1 – Information

For PTE writing task 1, you will need to write a summary of a brief academic text. The text will usually be 200 to 250 words in length, and a high-level summary of it should be a complex, well-developed sentence that is 50 to 75 words long. You are allowed 10 minutes to complete the task.

Writing Task 1 Tips

- First read the text quickly and identify the main topic.
- Then identify and note down the most important points.
- Write two sentences to summarize the information.
- Then join the two sentences into one sentence by using subordination, coordination, and modifying phrases.
- Remember not to copy exact phrases from the text. You must find your own words using synonyms or antonyms.

Example: Now look at the following example text and try to summarize it. Then look at the example response and further tips on the next page.

The Middle Ages was a time of significant social and political change. As a result of the Germanic invasion in the fifth century, the autocratic system of Roman government was overthrown. In its place today is a collection of independent democratic nations. However, this development would not have been possible without the foundations laid throughout the Middle Ages.

Indeed, a productive process lay beneath many seemingly every-day, banal activities during this era. New societies began to materialize as the German invaders became acquainted with the Roman inhabitants. This intermingling of nationalities and ethnic groups was an important process that should not be overlooked because this type of hybridity bears a great deal of resemblance to the ethnic diversity of certain communities in modern society.

Nevertheless, this period also witnessed the rise in imperialism, defined as a political system in which a king or queen has absolute power. While many kings strived to rule in accordance with the law, some rulers treated their citizens harshly, without following established legal restrictions.

When the attitudes of people towards their rulers changed, the balance of power in the political system began to shift. To a significant extent, these changes influenced the functioning of present-day political systems.

3-Step Summary Writing Guide

1. First identify the main topic and the key points. These have been underlined in the sample below:

The <u>Middle Ages</u> was a time of significant social and political change. As a result of the <u>Germanic invasion</u> in the fifth century, the autocratic system of <u>Roman government was overthrown</u>. In its place today is a collection of independent democratic nations. However, this development would not have been possible without the foundations laid throughout the Middle Ages.

Indeed, a productive process lay beneath many seemingly every-day, banal activities during this era. <u>New societies</u> began to materialize as the German invaders became acquainted with the Roman inhabitants. This <u>intermingling</u> of nationalities and ethnic groups was an important process that should not be overlooked because this type of hybridity bears a great deal of <u>resemblance to</u> the ethnic diversity of certain communities in <u>modern society</u>.

Nevertheless, this period also witnessed the rise in <u>imperialism</u>, defined as a political system in which a king or queen has absolute power. While many kings strived to rule in accordance with the law, <u>some rulers treated their citizens harshly</u>, without following established legal restrictions.

When the <u>attitudes of people towards their rulers changed,</u> the balance of power in the political system began to shift. To a significant extent, these changes <u>influenced</u> the functioning of <u>present-day political systems</u>.

---

2. Now write two sentences. The first sentence below summarizes paragraphs 1 and 2, and the second sentence summarizes paragraphs 3 and 4.

The balance of power shifted in the Middle Ages as Roman rule was ended by German conquerors, causing increased ethnic diversity and the socialization of new, more plural communities that resemble our contemporary society.

Imperialism advanced during this time, but the public rebelled when some rulers behaved tyrannically, and this laid the foundations for the development of our modern government and society.

3. Now combine the two sentences into one complex, well-developed sentence for your final answer.

The balance of power shifted in the Middle Ages as Roman rule was ended by German conquerors, leading to increased ethnic diversity and the socialization of new, more plural communities that resemble our contemporary society, as well as a public reaction against the concomitant advance of tyrannical forms of imperialism, a rebellion which laid the foundations for the development of our modern government.

PTE Writing Task 2 – Information and Tips

For Task 2, you will be asked to write an essay on a given topic. You may need to write an argumentative or opinion-based essay for this task.

You are allowed 20 minutes to complete the task, and you are advised to spend 5 minutes planning your essay and 15 minutes writing and checking it. Your response should be 200 to 300 words long.

Task 2 Essay Structure

- **Number of Paragraphs:** Your essay should consist of four or five paragraphs.

- **Development and Grammar:** Your sentences should be long and well-developed, and your writing should be grammatically correct.

- **Introduction:** In the first paragraph, you should restate the issue and provide some background information on it. You should also provide a thesis statement that explains the position you are going to take in the essay.

- **Main Body:** You should then write two or three main body paragraphs, each of which should be devoted to one of your supporting points.

- **Conclusion:** Your final paragraph should be a conclusion that sums up the viewpoints you have expressed in the main body. Your conclusion may sometimes have a forward-looking aspect, such as proposing a solution or making a prediction.

- **High-Level Vocabulary:** You will also need to use high-level, advanced vocabulary in order to receive a high score on this task. To improve your vocabulary, please see our separate publication entitled:

  PTE Academic Vocabulary Practice Book with Exercises and Answers: Review of Advanced Vocabulary for the Speaking, Writing, Reading, and Listening Sections of the Pearson English Test

Sample Writing Task 2 – Instructions

Read the essay topic below and write an essay about it. Your response should be no more than 300 words in length. Give reasons and examples to support your viewpoints.

When you have finished, compare your responses to the sample essay on the following page. Then study the comments below the essay sample.

Task 2:

With the rise in the availability of online information and services, many people would now consider life without the internet unfathomable. Yet, others believe that the internet is full of too much unreliable and false information.

Does the internet contain too much dubious material or is it genuinely something that we now cannot live without?

PTE Writing Task 2 – Sample Essay

Many people believe that the internet is essential for communication in our modern society. On the other hand, there are those who hold the view that the internet contains worthless or **offensive** information. This essay will show that although the internet needs to be used cautiously in certain circumstances, it also contains some helpful educational materials and factual data.

It is true that internet usage needs to be approached **vigilantly** on certain occasions. For example, parents worry about children accessing websites that contain violent, illegal, or sexual materials. This, in turn, could negatively influence the **formative** years of a child's personality development. In addition, some information on the internet needs to be read with a **critical** mind. The qualifications of the site owner, as well as the accuracy and quality of the information on the site need to be **scrutinized** skeptically.

In spite of these **caveats**, the internet is also practical for our daily lives. First of all, it makes some daily tasks more convenient, such as booking airline tickets and making other travel arrangements.

There are also websites that contain **indispensable** factual information. Consider the case of someone who wants to quit smoking. He or she can use any search engine to find webpages that offer help and advice with this situation. In addition, many of these types of websites are established by governmental agencies or charitable organizations, so the user can be confident that the information contained on these webpages is trustworthy.

To sum up, there are of course some situations in which users of the internet need to be **prudent**. Yet, there are also many helpful and accurate websites as well. It is up to each adult individual or parent, in the case of children, to decide which websites they are going to access. [297 words]

Essay Analysis and Further Tips

The previous essay is high level for the following reasons:

1) It demonstrates excellent topic development. Each paragraph contains reasons and examples to support the student's point of view.

2) It is well organized. Notice the words and phrases that are <u>underlined</u>, which the student uses to make the essay flow well.

3) The essay is grammatically correct. Notice that essays for writing task 2 often use verbs in the simple present or present perfect tenses. These tenses are needed because you will often be asked to write about a topic of recent importance.

4) The essay contains high-level academic vocabulary. Please notice the words in **bold**. Try to learn these words if you don't know them already, as well as other advanced vocabulary.

5) It has well-developed, long sentences and is nearly 300 words in length.

PTE Writing Practice Test 1

Instructions: Read items 1 and 2 below and write a one-sentence summary of each one. You have ten minutes each to complete these tasks. Each of your summaries should contain 75 words or less. When you have finished, compare your responses to the sample summaries on the following pages.

Item 1

Employers use a range of different methods to recruit employees, and employees use a range of different methods to look for work. Where people who are looking for work are using the same methods as employers are using to seek employees, then a match between the two is likely. However, this is not always obvious to either party, which limits the efficiency of the job-matching process.

If there is balance in the local labor market, employers will be able to find employees easily and people seeking work will be able to find jobs quickly. At the same time, the market price of jobs paid through wages and earnings should arguably be stable or rise in line with national trends.

Where employers cannot fill their vacancies with workers of the desired caliber, they may report to surveys that they have "hard-to-fill vacancies" or "skill-shortage vacancies" and might also respond by raising the earnings offered to potential recruits. Frequently, the earnings of existing workers can also rise as increased overtime is paid. In the same way that motorists will pay increased prices for fuel when petrol supplies are scarce, rising earnings above the national or local average will indicate some degree of excess employer demand over labor supply in the local area.

Item 2

Many cities, towns, and villages around the world are becoming increasingly vigilant about computer and television recycling in order to protect the environment and avoid possible soil contamination. Because computers contain many parts that can readily release toxins into the soil, city governments are seeking alternative ways to dispose of antiquated computers and other types of discarded electronic equipment. This eventually will become a normal practice as more cities become aware of the potential danger of disposing of computers and other electronic products in landfills. Activist groups are also informing the public about computer recycling and are researching new and better ways to dispose of electronic equipment.

In many cities, local electronic stores or recycling centers will take disused computers and other electronics, dismantle them, and place the parts into the correct containers for disposal. This method of disposal will soon become a necessity on a global scale as the computer industry perpetually upgrades operating systems, in effect thereby effectively establishing the circumstances under which consumers need to replace old computers in order to keep their equipment and related software up-to-date. If obsolete computers continue to be placed into landfills as they have in the past, this situation will eventually cause environmental issues that will need to be addressed by the government.

Instructions: Read the essay topics in items 3 and 4 below and write essays about each one. Your responses should be no more than 300 words in length. Give reasons and examples to support your viewpoints.

You are allowed 20 minutes for each essay.

When you have finished, compare your responses to the sample essays on the pages following the essay prompts.

Item 3:

Some parents are grateful to have television programs that help to entertain their children and keep them occupied. However, others fear that certain programs on television may be harmful for children.

Should children be allowed to watch whatever they like on television or are parents right to be concerned about the potential dangers of television programs?

Item 4:

By filling the atmosphere with exhaust from cars and other vehicles, humans can be said "to distill the poison that blights the paradise they seek" (F. Olmsted). Indeed, pollution is increasing on a global level, and certain countries already have measures in place to combat this problem.

Should the government intervene in the problem of vehicle pollution or should individuals be free to use their own personal forms of automated transport as they wish?

Item 1 – Sample Response

Organizations and job-seekers use various methods, which are usually quick and effective, to offer and seek work and to match employees with employers. However, there are shortcomings in the current system, including imbalances in labor markets, volatility in the market rates for employment, and scarcity of qualified employees, which causes rising labor prices due to the excess demand for labor over the limited supply of labor.

Item 2 – Sample Response

The disposal of ever-increasing amounts of antiquated computers and electronics caused by constant upgrades from suppliers and demand from consumers has become a pressing global problem, and several solutions have been created in order to avoid the ground pollution caused when the noxious substances contained within these devices escape into the soil, including research and information dissemination by activists, the establishment of earmarked recycling venues, and possible government intervention over the longer term.

Item 3 – Sample Essay

Televisual media has become a pervasive force in the lives of families around the world today. Yet, a central question remains regarding whether watching television is harmful or beneficial for children. An analysis of this question reveals that television programs present three major concerns in the case of children, including depictions of violence, the use of profane language, and the representation of poor moral role models.

Television programs that portray violence are a paramount concern for parents nowadays. Recent research has shown that children may commit acts of violence because they wish to emulate the behavior that they see on television. This is true whether these violent acts are portrayed by well-known actors or comic book figures.

Television programs that contain profane or disrespectful language also worry parents with young children. Because any form of censorship has become out of vogue, it is now very common for television programs to show characters expressing impolite, rude, and insulting utterances to one another. Bearing resemblance to the case of portrayals of violence, these depictions might also be inimical to child development.

Finally, some parents are upset about the moral behavior depicted on television. As they struggle to teach their children ethical values, parents might despair about the lack of morals and ethics represented in some of the so-called role models on television. For instance, certain characters not only have no remorse for their cruel actions, but also frequently go unpunished by larger society.

Because of these factors, many parents believe that television programs send their youth the wrong kinds of messages. The potential emulation of this poor behavior by their children is something they wish to avoid at all costs, and they have accordingly decided to restrict television in their households for these reasons. [292 words]

Item 4 – Sample Essay

There is a constant question in society nowadays about the environmental and health risks caused by the use of motorized vehicles. It is irrefutable that increasing regulatory measures would bring about benefits to society. This essay will discuss two measures that the government might take to address the issue.

There is no doubt that countries using non-motorized transport as a norm have a better level of health in the general population. In Denmark, where most people cycle to work, it is reported that levels of heart disease and stroke are far lower than they are in other countries. We only need to look at remote villages that do not have automotive traffic to see how negatively motorized vehicles have affected other areas of our planet.

The levels of air pollution and other forms of environmental contamination are far less in these villages than in so-called "developed" countries. Consider the converse case, for instance, in the United States, where a heavy reliance on motor vehicles has resulted in this country being one of the largest emitters of greenhouse gases in the world.

Perhaps the best intervention would be to have the government provide certain incentives to those who decide not to use motorized vehicles. For instance, the government could offer rebates or subsidies on bicycle purchases. Another possible course of action would be to introduce certain fees or fines for vehicle usage, but to establish those controls within very clear limits.

To sum up, one thing is clear: whether by positive reinforcement, as in the first example, or by negative reinforcement as in the second, both schemes take into account the pressing concern of the state of the global environment, as well as protecting the needs of the population for personal health and individual freedom. [294 words]

PTE Reading Practice Test 1

You are allowed 40 minutes for the reading test. When you have finished, compare your answers to those in the answer key.

Instructions: For items 1 and 2, read the passage and choose the correct answer. *Only one* response is correct for each question.

Item 1

According to Stephen Krashen's input hypothesis, a language learner improves his or her language skills when he or she is exposed to language input such as lectures or reading materials that are one level above the learner's current level of language ability. Language output such as verbal or written expressions are not seen to have any direct relationship to the learner's ability.

1.   Which of the following most accurately defines the input hypothesis?
    A. It is an assumption that all language learners begin at the same level of ability.
    B. It is a theory which asserts that learners can best improve their language skills when their learning is appropriately challenging.
    C. It is a school of thought that discounts the importance of traditional grammatical skills.
    D. It is a system of language rules established by Stephen Krashen that learners of new languages try to follow.

Go on to the next page.

Item 2

The civil order control function suggests that public order is best maintained through agencies other than the police force or militia. The constitutions of many countries now make provisions for the introduction of martial law, allowing it only in cases of national emergency or in the case of threats to national security from foreign countries. In democratic nations, severe restrictions are imposed on the implementation of martial law, meaning that a formal declaration of military rule over a nation should be rendered virtually impractical. In spite of these democratic systems being in place, forms of military control are still instituted during times of crisis, with a country's military system being mobilized to support civil authorities, such as municipalities and local police forces. The Department of Defense recently commented: "The use of military force to control the population is still a necessary albeit inimical outcome for the governments of certain countries around the globe today."

2.   What point is the writer making in this paragraph?
      A.   The declaration of martial law is sometimes needed, although it is usually undesirable.
      B.   The country's military system should provide more support for civil authorities.
      C.   The police forces of most municipalities are already over-burdened with other tasks.
      D.   Martial law should automatically be established during times of national crisis.

Instructions: For items 3 and 4, read the passage and choose the correct answer. *More than one* response is correct for each question.

Item 3

Do mice really prefer cheese to all other foodstuffs? One well-known exterminating company has demonstrated how best to catch these pesky rodents: lemon-flavored candy. It appears that the confection has a double advantage. Its sweet smell attracts the mouse much more strongly than does cheese, and its sticky consistency helps to hold the creature captive for the moment it takes for the trap to release. Through logical analogy, we can therefore conclude that it is fallacious to presume that other groups of animals have preferences for certain food groups. For instance, we cannot readily conclude that all dogs would choose meat or that all cats would select milk as their favorite foodstuffs.

3.   Which of the following is true according to the passage?
    A. Mice are attracted more to the texture of the candy than to its smell.
    B. Some animals have a very acute sense of smell.
    C. Many scientific experiments demonstrate that dogs do not prefer the taste and texture of meat to the taste and texture of other food.
    D. Mice can be caught with lemon-flavored candy more easily than they can be caught with cheese.
    E. One cannot conclude that animals crave foods based merely on stereotypes.

Item 4

Acid has been present in rain for millennia, naturally occurring from volcanoes and plankton. However, scientific research shows that the acid content of rain has increased dramatically over the past two hundred years, in spite of humanity's recent attempts to control the problem. Rain consists of two elements, nitrogen and sulfur. When sulfur is burned, it transforms into sulfur dioxide. Nitrogen also oxides when burned. When released from factories into the atmosphere, both sulfur dioxide and nitrogen oxide react with the water molecules in rain to form sulfuric acid and nitric acid, respectively. Factories and other enterprises have built high chimneys in an attempt to carry these gases away from urban areas. Nevertheless, the effect of the structures has been to spread the gases more thinly and widely in the atmosphere, thereby exacerbating the problem. The acid in rain also emanates from automobile exhaust, domestic residences, and power stations. The latter have been the culprit of the bulk of the acid in rainwater in recent years. Since the pollutants are carried by the wind, countries can experience acid rain from pollution that was generated in countries thousands of miles away.

4.   Which of the following statements can be supported from this text?
    A. When sulfur dioxide is ignited, it turns into sulfur.
    B. Sulfuric acid and nitric acid are created when sulfur dioxide and nitrogen oxide react with rain water.
    C. Chimneys have been effective in solving the problem of acid rain.
    D. Pollution from vehicles is one contributor to acid rain.
    E. Countries are safe from pollution that is created several thousand miles away.

Instructions: The sentences in item 5 and item 6 below are in a random order. Number the sentences in each item to indicate their correct order.

Item 5

_____ (A) After studying under both Mozart and Haydn, Beethoven became a virtuoso pianist and had many wealthy patrons, who supported him financially.

_____ (B) His most expressive works are considered to be his fifth and sixth symphonies and his opera entitled *Fidelio*.

_____ (C) Ludwig von Beethoven was one of the most influential figures in the development of musical forms during the Classical period.

_____ (D) However, Beethoven's compositions express the creative energy of the artist himself.

_____ (E) Other composers created music that would merely suit the demands of these patrons.

Item 6

_____ (A) Ground and aerial surveys were conducted only slightly in advance of the construction of the road due to the snow, and the survey teams worked just miles ahead of the construction crew in some cases.

_____ (B) Swampland along the route was a further complication, and efforts to avoid the waterlogged ground created many bends in the road.

_____ (C) The first step in completing the mammoth project was to plan the exact route that the road was going to take before construction even started.

_____ (D) Apart from the challenges inherent in building a road in such inclement conditions, bridges had to be erected and culverts had to be laid in drainage ditches.

_____ (E) A true feat of modern engineering, the Alaska Highway was constructed to link Edmonton in Alberta, Canada, to Fairbanks, Alaska.

Instructions: Each of the four following passages in items 7 to 10 contains missing words. Choose the correct word for each gap from the list below each passage.

Item 7

Gibberellins are a (1) _____ group of plant hormones that are involved in many botanical processes. Commonly used in combination with (2) _____ botanical hormones called auxins, their primary function is to promote (3) _____ plant growth by accelerating the elongation of cells. They also aid in the formation of fruit and seed, as well as delay aging in leaves. Having become important for (4) _____ reasons in recent years, the hormones are also used to help meet the ever-growing demand for new hybrids of hardy plants and (5) _____ flowers.

similar / beautiful / rapid / capricious / complex / commercial / high / like

---

Item 8

The notion of liberal arts education is believed to have been established in ancient Greece. (1) _____ the disciplines of logic, rhetoric, and grammar, a liberal arts education in those days was designed to train (2) _____ of society to undertake important civic duties, such as jury service and public debate. In modern parlance, the term "liberal arts education" can be (3) _____ in a variety of ways, although it is generally taken to mean that the (4) _____ will include courses in one or more of the subject areas of the humanities, such as languages, literature, or philosophy.

interpreted / members / including / invented / studies / consisting / people

---

Item 9

The (1) _____ of the president of the General Assembly on the Declaration of Human Rights was a great event in the life of the United Nations. This declaration has become the international Magna Carta of all people everywhere. Its proclamation by the General Assembly was an event comparable to the (2) _____ of the Bill of Rights by the people of the United States and the adoption of comparable declarations at different times in other (3) _____ . (Adaptation of "Adoption of the Declaration of Human Rights" by Eleanor Roosevelt)

nation / approval / event / countries / circumstance / signature

Item 10

The Higgs mechanism is the process in quantum field theory whereby symmetry is broken down, leading to (1) _____ particles. Quantum field theory alone tells us that all particles should be massless. Yet, groundbreaking (2) _____ research has found that particles can acquire mass when the symmetry of energy within a system is less than that of the interaction governing the system. Although they have never even seen this particle, scientists understand theoretically that the Higgs particle is a by-product of the acquisition of mass by other particles. Discovering this (3) _____ particle remains one of the (4) _____ challenges of modern-day particle physicists.

elusive / greatest / massive / clever / scientific / insignificant / unknown

Instructions: Each of the following passages in items 11 to 15 contains missing words. Choose the correct word for each gap from the answer choices provided below each passage.

Item 11

For every building that is successfully constructed, there are countless others that have never received the chance to (1) _____ the drawing board. Some of these unbuilt structures were practical and mundane, while others expressed the flights of fancy of the architect. Known to us today only through the (2) _____ left on paper, many unbuilt buildings were originally designed to commemorate particular people or events. Such was the (3) _____ with the monument dubbed the *Beacon of Progress*, which was to be erected in Chicago to display exhibits dedicated to great Americans in history. However, scholar Samantha Mulholland points out that other (4) _____ projects were far more (5) _____, like that of *The Floating Spheres*, described as (6) _____ held aloft by hot air to house cities of the future.

Gap 1

A. get   B. take   C. leave   D. find

Gap 2

A. words   B. plans   C. notes   D. writing

Gap 3

A. case   B. behavior   C. situation   D. event

Gap 4

A. wanted   B. known   C. included   D. proposed

Gap 5

A. useful   B. welcome   C. impractical   D. servile

Gap 6

A. clouds   B. balloons   C. buildings   D. structures

Item 12

There has been a fundamental change in the (1) _____ between the actor and the audience in recent years. According to Aristotelian principles, actors should provoke an (2) _____ catharsis in the members of the audience. Traditionally, actors have provided this release of feeling, but this is far from the case in the performances in many of today's (3) _____ motion pictures and television programs. Even though many productions are increasingly based on contrived stories or weak plots, modern actors could do more with these roles than merely create mindless diversions. Sadly, the work of many performers nowadays lacks gravitas. When actors engage in vacuous (4) _____ like these, they do not even begin to serve the higher purpose of their profession.

Gap 1

A. conversation　　　B. dialogue　　　C. relationship　　　D. instructions

Gap 2

A. emotional　　　B. mental　　　C. physical　　　D. biological

Gap 3

A. daily　　　B. modern　　　C. former　　　D. previous

Gap 4

A. engagements　　　B. tasks　　　C. work　　　D. performances

Item 13

The ancient Egyptians used eye shadow over 5,000 years ago. The cosmetic was applied for personal beautification, as well as for practical reasons. (1) _____ from a paste of malachite, a copper salt that was bright green, the eye paint protected against glare from the sun, in addition to being an (2) _____ color. On her upper eye lids, Cleopatra wore blue eye shadow made of ground lapis lazuli stone, much like other women of her day. The queen used green malachite as an accent below her eyes, and kohl, which (3) _____ of lead sulfide, to provide color to her eyelashes and eyebrows. Red ochre, iron-based clay, provided her with lip and cheek color. Henna, a reddish-brown dye that was derived from a bush, was also commonly used by women in those days as a nail polish. (4) _____ with tannin from the bark or fruit of various trees in order to be heavy enough for cosmetic use, henna was not used only by women. Men also used the substance to darken their hair and beards.

Gap 1

A. Contained   B. Composed   C. Made   D. Consisted

Gap 2

A. attractive   B. onerous   C. inventive   D. unique

Gap 3

A. included   B. consisted   C. derived   D. provided

Gap 4

A. Tainted   B. Flavored   C. Composed   D. Thickened

Item 14

Recent research shows that technology and social media platforms may actually be making us (1) _____. Survey results indicate that many people would prefer to interact on Facebook or Instagram, rather than see friends and family in person. The primary reason cited for this (2) _____ was that one does not need to go to the effort to dress up and travel in order to use these social media platforms. Another independent survey revealed that people often remain glued to their hand-held devices to check their social media when they do go out with friends. So, it seems that social media platforms may be adversely (3) _____ our social skills and interpersonal relationships. Yet, resulting from the success of WAP (Wireless Application Protocol) in smart phones and hand-held devices, wireless technology can create more efficiency in our day-to-day lives. These technologies help to make the mobile information society happen by (4) _____ the boundaries between home, the office, and the outside world. The seamless integration and connectivity that wireless technology brings with it make it possible to work more efficiently. Business users can explore a wide range of interactive services which were difficult to envisage years ago because of the complexity previously involved in making such devices communicate with each other.

Gap 1

A. antisocial   B. miserable   C. isolated   D. upset

Gap 2

A. cause   B. phenomenon   C. result   D. indication

Gap 3

A. causing   B. improving   C. affecting   D. resulting

Gap 4

A. making   B. creating   C. drawing   D. blurring

Item 15

Today archaeologists are still endeavoring to uncover the secrets of Africa's past. Evidence of the earliest human activity has been found in the south and east of the (1) _____, where climatic conditions helped to preserve the human skeletons and stone tools found there. Genetic science confirms that these are quite likely the oldest remains in the world of modern people, with this classification (2) _____ on the ability of humans to become adaptable and ready to respond to environmental change. Even though the artifacts and skeletons of early Africans are most commonly found in a highly fragmented state, these (3) _____ are more than sufficient in order to make a number of significant conclusions. Perhaps the most important discovery is that there is great variation among the human remains, indicating a wide array of physical differences among members of the population. While the early population was diverse, it has been well established that the earliest species of hominids spread from Africa to other continents. The first traces of human technology, consisting of simple stone tools, were also discovered in Africa. Having been (4) _____ long before the invention of metallurgy, tools had gradually been made smaller and more sophisticated. Microliths, fine stone tools that were fitted to handles, were used as cutting and scraping tools and may even have been the precursor to the bow and arrow.

Gap 1

A. state   B. nation   C. location   D. continent

Gap 2

A. made   B. based   C. proposed   D. sustained

Gap 3

A. groups   B. evidence   C. findings   D. demonstrations

Gap 4

A. developed   B. found   C. discovered   D. discussed

PTE Listening Practice Test 1

Please see the answer key for sample summaries and answers.

To access the recording for this practice test, open the link entitled "Listening Practice Test 1" at:

pte-listening.examsam.com

All of the appropriate timings are provided in the recording, so you may listen to it continuously without stopping if you would like to simulate actual exam conditions.

Item 1:

You will hear a brief class discussion. Write a 50 to 70-word summary of what you have heard. After the recording finishes, you are allowed 10 minutes to complete your summary.

Item 2:

You will hear a short excerpt from a lecture. Write a 50 to 70-word summary of what you have heard. After the recording finishes, you are allowed 10 minutes to complete your summary.

Item 3:

Listen to the recording and choose the correct answers. More than one answer is correct.

Which of the following statements are true?

    A. Most composers studied abroad during their careers in the 18th century.
    B. Baroque music developed and expanded during the 18th century.
    C. Bach, Handel, and Beethoven composed new musical works.
    D. Some composers became less popular with the public during this time.
    E. Music had much more romantic feeling in the 18th century.

Item 4:

Listen to the recording and choose the correct answers. More than one answer is correct.

    A. Tomato genes have recently been inserted into cold-water fish.
    B. Gene splicing has been used in both plants and in human subjects.
    C. Experiments have been conducted involving gene splicing, all of which have been controversial.
    D. Research with sheep has been used to help those suffering from a blood disorder.
    E. Scientists in Scotland received praise for their work with Factor 9.

Item 5:

Listen to the recording and fill in the missing words in the text below.

The roots of some plants can go (1) _____ deep into the soil. In fact, the roots of some plants (2) _____ nearly one hundred feet below ground. However, roots can (3) _____ in the most unusual places, including the air. The roots from the banyan tree in southern Asia grow (4) _____ from the tree until they reach the ground and anchor into the earth. The banyan tree therefore starts (5) _____ as an air plant before its roots grow underground. (6) _____, not every part of a plant located below ground is a root. The black locust tree, for instance, sends up sprouts from underground. These sprouts do not come from roots, but rather from underground (7) _____ called rhizomes.

Item 6:

Listen to the recording and fill in the missing words in the text below.

Group projects at college are sometimes assigned in order to promote teamwork and (1) _____ communication skills. When the teacher sets a group project, students are required to work together in small groups in order to achieve the (2) _____ outcome. Yet, in my experience, students rarely work together in such an idealistic, (3) _____ manner. Rather, the one or two responsible students in the group will be left to complete the project, while others (4) _____ their responsibility. I am opposed to the use group projects for (5) _____ purposes since non-motivated students often perform very few of the required tasks and attempt to take credit for the work of the more capable students.

Item 7:

Select the answer that best relates to the recording. Only one answer is correct.

A. Languages around the world affect writers since new words and phrases are introduced into their work from these languages.
B. Clichés develop when phrases are introduced into a language and become widely used. Authors have been responsible for a number of such popular phrases.
C. Stories from authors are popular in society. When writers promote their own work, phrases are introduced into a language.
D. Sentimental uses of words and phrases exist in every language. Quotations from Benjamin Franklin and Shakespeare are examples of this.

Item 8:

Select the answer that best relates to the recording. Only one answer is correct.

A. Various seismic events occur around the world, but the occurrence of these events is very infrequent.
B. Motion in an epicenter causes earthquakes to occur. This can lead to devastating loss of property and life.
C. The importance of earthquake prediction systems cannot be understated since members of the public are very ill-informed about them.
D. Earthquakes occur due to shifts in geological features. There is an ever-present possibility of earthquakes, so predicting these phenomena is very important.

Item 9:

Listen to the recording and choose the correct answer. Only one answer is correct.

What is the speaker mainly attempting to express in his comments?

A. Many students have complained about the noise in Henderson Hall.
B. The noise in the library is counterproductive and unacceptable.
C. The student would like to move into different accommodation.
D. Henderson Hall is simply too far from the library to be practical.

Item 10:

Listen to the recording and choose the correct answer. Only one answer is correct.

What is the main idea of this lecture?

    A. The process by which reflexes create involuntary action.
    B. The way that electrical impulses function on pathways.
    C. Sensory neurons and their relationship to motor neurons.
    D. The relationship of reflexes to external stimuli.

Item 11:

At the end of the recording, a beep has been substituted for the final word or words. Select the correct word or words to replace the beep.

    A. robbed people
    B. was a real person
    C. lived in England
    D. is worth studying

Item 12:

At the end of the recording, a beep has been substituted for the final word or words. Select the correct word or words to replace the beep.

    A. with plastic
    B. for durability
    C. by the ground

Item 13:

The text of a recording is provided below. Some of the words in the text do not match the recording. Please identify the words that are different.

The basement of the building was made watertight by constructing massive concrete walls, which were built on site section-by-section. Because the ground was so soft, finding the solid land below was an immense undertaking. This was accomplished by utilizing a dredging appliance to dig a narrow trench. This trench was kept full of heavy clay during its construction to prevent it from falling in. Then, the trench was dug to a depth of thirty-six meters. More trenches were put in place until the site was completely enclosed on its sides. Ultimately, the underground concrete wall that functioned as the basement of the building was the height of a twelve-story building. Next, the concrete upper floor of the building was constructed so that work above ground could commence. During the next phase of completion, eight giant steel columns, which weighed more than a thousand tons, were erected to support the walls of the structure.

Item 14:

The text of a recording is provided below. Some of the words in the text do not match the recording. Please identify the words that are different.

The study of the psychology of human nature is often regarded as an investigation into the meaning of life. This subject usually deals with four key problematical areas: human choice, human thought, human personality, and the unity of the human being. The first problem area, human choice, asks whether human beings can actually make decisions that can change their futures. In the second problem area, human thought, epistemology is considered. Epistemology means the study of knowledge; it should not be confounded with ontology, the study of being or existence. The third key issue, human personality, takes a look at emotional, spiritual, and community elements. Importantly, the study of the communal asset focuses on community and communication, rather than on government or the philosophy of the state. Finally, the fourth problem, the unification of the human being, explores the first three areas more fully and asks when there is any unifying basis for human choice, thought, and personality.

For items 15 to 17, write down the sentences you hear. You need to write each sentence exactly as it is spoken. Write as much as of each sentence as you possibly can. You will hear each sentence only once.

Item 15:

Item 16:

Item 17:

PTE Academic Practice Test 2

The lecture texts, correct answers, and suggested responses for all of the items are included in the answer key at the end of the book.

Now open the recording entitled "Speaking Practice Test 2" at:

pte-listening.examsam.com

Follow the instructions on the recording as you attempt the practice test that follows.

Speaking Practice Test 2

Read Aloud

For items 1 to 6, read the text aloud as clearly and as naturally as you can, at a good pace, and with good pronunciation and emphasis.

Item 1:

There are various estimates of the number of countries in the world, depending upon how a country or nation state is defined. Most estimates indicate that there are nearly 200 countries on our planet, in addition to the territories that claim independence through self-declaration or territorial autonomy by having their own leaderships, flags, postage stamps, and military systems.

Item 2:

First aid is the management and treatment of a victim of injury at the site of an accident or incident. Whether the patient is conscious or unconscious, it is important to check for respiration and heartbeat, to limit any bleeding, and to handle any wounds as gently as possible. Tea, alcohol, coffee or other fluids should not be administered, nor should any food be provided for consumption.

Item 3:

The word "investments" in economics is chiefly assigned to two different but related enterprises. The first is the acquisition of assets in order to generate income or other productive gains, such as placing money in a bank or purchasing stocks, while the second is the creation of investments such as equipment, factories, buildings, and other structures or works in progress.

Item 4:

A black box is a complete unit in a computer or electronic system whose internal function need not be understood by the user in order to operate it. The term is commonly used to refer to the data recorder in aircraft which collects information about the plane's performance during a flight and which can be utilized to investigate the cause of a crash.

Item 5:

There are a number of schemes presently in use to divide the Earth into regions by climate, based on average annual temperature, mean monthly temperature, and total snow or rainfall. Although land position generally determines the amount of sunshine any region receives, elevation is what most greatly affects snow and rainfall.

Item 6:

Natural laws in science are descriptive laws which attempt to explain the behavior of objects at rest or in motion in the physical world. However, within the legal system, natural law is said to define how people ought to behave, and is rooted in ethics, philosophy, and the observation of human nature.

Repeat the Sentence

For items 7 to 16, repeat each sentence exactly as it is recorded. You will hear each sentence only once.

Describe the Image

For items 17 to 22, describe each illustration in detail. You are allowed 25 seconds to study each illustration, and then you will need to speak for 40 seconds on each one to give your response.

Go on to the next page.

Item 17:

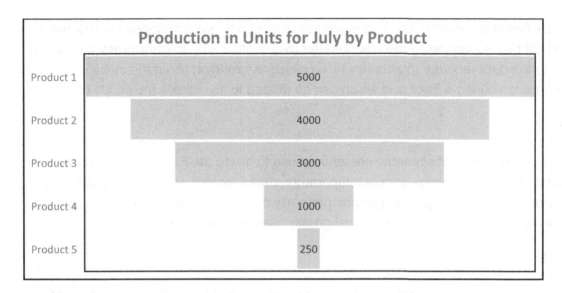

Production in Units for July by Product

Product 1	5000
Product 2	4000
Product 3	3000
Product 4	1000
Product 5	250

Item 18:

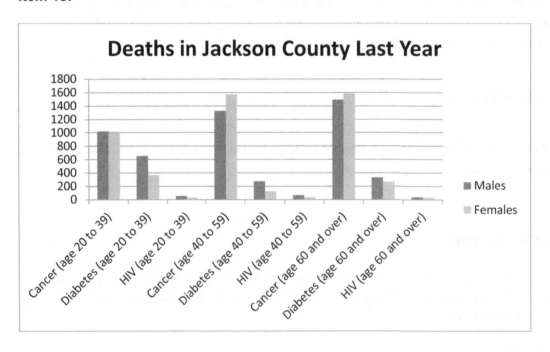

Deaths in Jackson County Last Year

Item 19:

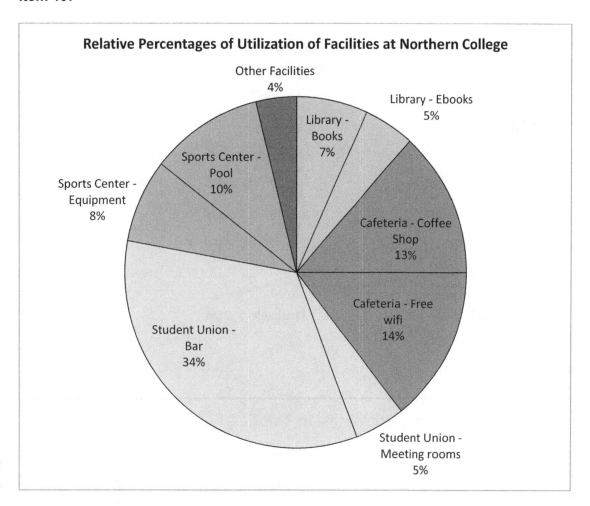

Relative Percentages of Utilization of Facilities at Northern College

- Other Facilities 4%
- Library - Books 7%
- Library - Ebooks 5%
- Cafeteria - Coffee Shop 13%
- Cafeteria - Free wifi 14%
- Student Union - Meeting rooms 5%
- Student Union - Bar 34%
- Sports Center - Equipment 8%
- Sports Center - Pool 10%

Go on to the next page.

Item 20:

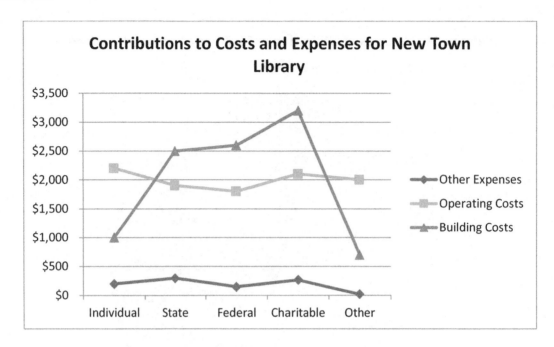

Item 21:

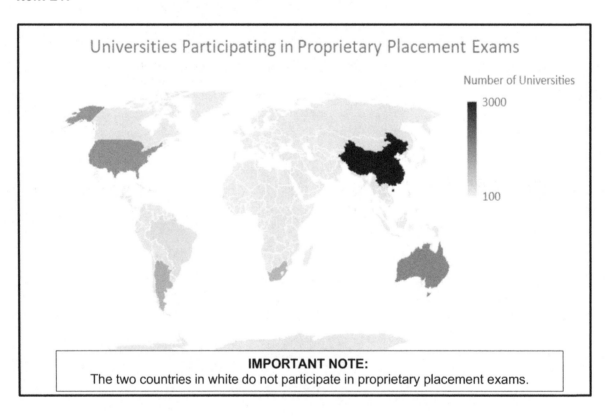

Item 22:

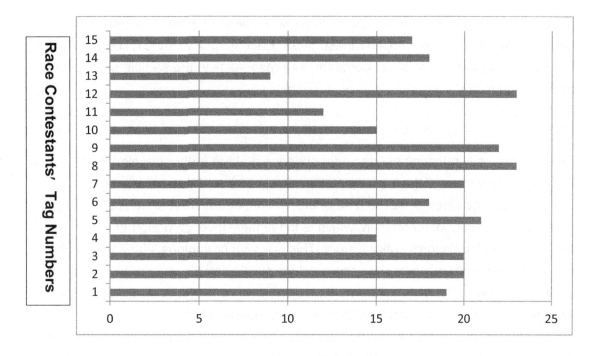

Time in Minutes

Re-tell Lecture

For items 23 to 25, you will hear talks or lectures. After listening to each one, you will have 10 seconds to review your notes. Then you will be given 40 seconds for each one to restate its contents.

Answer Short Question

For items 26 to 35, you will hear 10 questions. You need to give a brief answer of one or just a few words for each one. For these questions, you should speak immediately after the beep.

PTE Writing Practice Test 2

Instructions: Read items 1 and 2 and write a one-sentence summary of each one. You have ten minutes each to complete these tasks. Each response should contain 75 words or less. When you have finished, compare your responses to the sample summaries on the following pages.

Item 1

Ireland is currently pursuing energy independence and the further development of their robust economy through the implementation of research and development into alternative energy sources. At the time of this writing, nearly 90% of Ireland's energy needs are met through importation, which is the highest level of foreign product dependence in the nation's entire history. This is a very precarious situation, and the Irish government sharply perceives the need for developing alternative energy sources within their nation. The Irish government also seeks to conserve and rejuvenate its naturally beautiful environment and to clean up its atmosphere through the implementation of alternative energy supplies. The European Union has mandated a reduction in sulfuric and nitric oxide emissions for all member nations, and green energy is needed to meet these objectives. While hydroelectric power has been utilized in Ireland in some areas since the 1930's and has been very effective, much more hydroelectric infrastructure needs to be installed. The nation is attempting to utilize the wave power of the Atlantic Ocean on its west coast, which is a potential energy supply that Ireland would have in great store.

Item 2

From the embattled frontline of the book and printed media world, there seems to be nothing but bad news. Publishers have become besieged, and bookstores have fallen. Well-known literary agents are scurrying around in search of life-saving mergers, and advances for authors have all but evaporated. The celebrity memoir is going the way of the dinosaur, and digital downloads are the future. Libraries and the once well-used books within them, now comprehensively digitized, have become cemeteries with artifacts of a dying tradition. It was once conventional wisdom that book sales and the publishing market were recession-proof, but this belief no longer rings true. A perfect storm of economic and technological change has transformed the literary atmosphere more completely than at any time in living memory. However, books and other forms of printed media, from other points of view, are still something tangible to celebrate. Readers are more dynamic and discriminating than they have been for generations, and literary festivals are booming. The books themselves, with certain notable exceptions, are better printed, bound, and jacketed than ever before. When comparing volumes published decades ago to current publications, the contrast is shocking. Narrow margins, cheap paper, and hideous typography have all had comprehensive aesthetic makeovers.

Instructions: Read the essay topics in items 3 and 4 below and write essays about each one. Your responses should be no more than 300 words in length. Give reasons and examples to support your viewpoints.

You are allowed 20 minutes for each essay.

When you have finished, compare your responses to the sample essays on the following pages.

Item 3:

Advertising costs businesses billions of dollars around the world every year. While some people believe that the promotion of new products and services is valuable for society, others fear the potentially manipulative outcomes of advertisements.

Is advertising helpful to the public or does it merely convince people to buy unnecessary products?

Item 4:

Sadism is a word that is sometimes used to describe taking enjoyment in being cruel to others and observing their suffering. Many people believe that delighting in others' pain and sorrows is never morally acceptable.

Are there certain situations in which it could be considered acceptable to be satisfied with the suffering of another person or is this a behavior that human beings should avoid at all costs?

Item 1 – Sample Response

In a tenuous situation because of a historically-unprecedented amount of over-reliance upon imported fuel sources, Ireland is attempting to become self-sufficient in its energy needs by developing more renewable energy sources, such as hydroelectricity, thereby protecting the country's environmental beauty, improving air quality conditions, and meeting European Union mandates on curtailing noxious emissions.

Item 2 – Sample Response

Some people think that the future for books and other printed materials looks bleak due to the fact that a downturn in the economy and the rise of digital media has caused libraries to become under-used and publishers, booksellers, agents, autobiographers, and other writers to suffer financially, but others insist that readers are more diverse and astute and that the quality of books is far better than ever before.

Item 3 – Sample Essay

Advertising is a powerful force in today's materialistic, status-conscious society. Consumers are bombarded with advertising at every turn, from advertisements on television and radio, to outdoor advertising on electronic signs and even on buses. This essay will reveal that while much advertising serves only to drive mindless consumerism, certain forms of advertising do, in fact, serve useful purposes.

Most advertising that we see is arguably the attempt of large companies to persuade the general public to buy products that they do not really need or to create demand for other new unnecessary products. One only has to consider the amount of advertising for toys during children's TV programs to see this phenomenon in action.

However, many would argue that advertising nevertheless does provide information about products to consumers and the public. They assert that, rather than producing a false economy, the practice of advertising helps to perpetuate competition and free enterprise in the marketplace and ultimately brings the best prices to customers. Under this view, advertising helps to sell goods to a larger market; making products cheaper since they can be mass produced in order to meet demand.

In addition, public service advertisements like those that warn against the dangers of driving while intoxicated or failing to wear a seat belt are also extremely valuable. Admittedly, these kinds of advertisements can literally have a very sobering effect.

Some believe that the government should intervene to stamp down on the false or misleading claims that certain advertisers attempt to make, and in fact, a sea change

51

may be taking place already. For instance, some TV and magazine advertisements are now required to display notes in order to qualify their claims. Providing information like this that clearly states the limitations of products can only have a salutary effect.
[296 words]

Item 4 – Sample Essay

While feeling pleasure when others suffer is a human emotion which most of us would not be so quick to admit, there are occasions when it is socially acceptable to take pleasure in the pain of others. Punishment for crime is a situation when it is not considered untoward to experience satisfaction over the suffering of others. That is to say, although being pleased to see others stricken is normally not acceptable in a civilized society, there are exceptions to this general rule when others have broken society's norms.

Unfortunately, even in modern times we have seen despotic rulers who treat members of their societies harshly, and in such situations, the reactions of those subjected to these regimes is certainly socially justifiable. The most unfortunate of these persecuted individuals are submitted to unthinkable states of existence in which their lives may even be threatened. Because they are forced to live in such unimaginable conditions, those suffering such persecution must feel gratified when the dictator is deposed. Once a regime is overthrown, relief and satisfaction are sometimes even felt around the world.

Punishment for crime is another instance of the acceptability of taking pleasure in another's suffering. Criminal law has been established to ensure that offenders are justly punished for their crimes so that members of the community can feel satisfied because justice has been served when the offender is punished. In addition, punishing social wrongs can act as a deterrent to would-be criminals, thereby further reinforcing social norms.

Whereas taking delight in the misfortune of others is a trait that normally would not receive social approbation, the circumstances faced in war and crime fall outside this conventional social restriction. However, it is doubtful that joy over others' suffering will ever be considered a socially-desirable quality outside these situations. [299 words]

Reading Practice Test 2

You are allowed 40 minutes for the reading test. When you have finished, compare your answers to those in the answer key.

Instructions: For items 1 and 2, read the passage and choose the correct answer. *Only one* response is correct for each question.

Item 1

Highly concentrated radioactive waste is lethal and can remain so for thousands of years. Accordingly, the disposal of this material remains an issue in most energy-producing countries around the world. In the United States, for example, liquid forms of radioactive waste are usually stored in stainless-steel tanks. For extra protection, the tanks are double-walled and surrounded by a concrete covering that is one meter thick. This storage solution is also utilized the United Kingdom, in most cases. The potential future problem lies in the fact that nuclear waste generates heat as radioactive atoms decay, thereby creating a high risk of a radioactive leak.

1.   What point is the writer making in this paragraph?
    A. A radioactive leak would have disastrous consequences.
    B. The stainless-steel tanks only contain waste in liquid form.
    C. The storage solution is only viable on a short-term basis
    D. Heat is generated as radioactive atoms decay.

Go on to the next page.

Item 2

For any state to make sex a qualification that must always result in the disenfranchisement of one entire half of the people is a violation of the supreme law of the land. By it, the blessings of liberty are forever withheld from women and their female posterity. To them, this government has no just powers derived from the consent of the governed. To them, this government is not a democracy. It is not a republic. It is an odious aristocracy; a hateful oligarchy of sex; the oligarchs over the mother and sisters, the wife and daughters, of every household – which ordains all men sovereigns, all women subjects, carries dissension, discord, and rebellion into every home of the nation (Adapted from "On Women's Right to Vote" by Susan B. Anthony).

2.   Which of the following most accurately summarizes the opinion of the author of the text?
    A. The entire populace is disenfranchised because of this problem.
    B. The government is too powerful in people's lives.
    C. The situation she is speaking about is unfair and change is necessary.
    D. Dissension and rebellion are bound to increase about his issue.

Instructions: For items 3 and 4, read the passage and choose the correct answers. *More than one* response is correct for each question.

Item 3

Working in a run-down laboratory near Paris, Marie Curie worked around the clock to discover a radioactive element. When she finally captured her quarry, she named it radium after the Latin word meaning ray. She had spent the day blending chemical compounds which could be used to destroy unhealthy cells in the body. As she was about to retire to bed that evening, she decided to return to her lab. There she found that the chemical compound had become crystalized in the bowls and was emitting the elusive light that she sought. Inspired by the French scientist Henri Becquerel, Curie won the Nobel Prize for Chemistry for her discovery.

3.   Which of the following statements are true according to the passage?
    A. Marie Curie was an inventive and determined chemist.
    B. Marie Curie made many important discoveries during her illustrious career.
    C. Radium is effective in treating cancer because it emits a glowing light.
    D. Henri Becquerel's work had an influence on Currie's research.
    E. Marie Curie decided to crystalize her invention to create radium.

Item 4

Equating the whole history of the struggle of humankind to that of the class struggle, the social and political writings of Karl Marx have been the impetus of a great deal of change within society. According to Marxism, the political school of thought based on Marx's doctrines, the working class should strive to defeat capitalism, since capitalistic societies inherently have within them a dynamic that results in the wealthy ruling classes oppressing the masses. The nation state is seen as an instrument of class rule because it supports private capital and suppresses the common person through economic mechanisms, such as the taxation of wages. Because growth of private capital is stimulated by earning profits and extracting surplus value in the production process, wages have to be kept low, further oppressing the working class.

Since capitalism reduces the purchasing power of workers to consume the goods that they produce, Marx emphasized that capitalism inheres in a central contradiction. Under the tenets of Marxism, capitalism is therefore inherently unstable. Marx asserted that productive power ideally should be in the hands of the general public, which would cause class differences to vanish. These idealistic writings have had a huge impact on culture and politics; yet, many believe that Marx's work lacked the practical details needed to bring about the changes to the class structure that he envisaged.

4.   Which of the following statements about Marxism can be supported by this text?
    A. The writings of Karl Marx are of social and political importance.
    B. Marxist views on capitalism have no consequences for private capital.
    C. Marxism claims that the class structure is inimical and oppressive for many people.
    D. Taxation and business profits cause wages to be increased.
    E. The work of Karl Marx has many practical applications.

Instructions: The sentences in item 5 and item 6 below are in a random order. Number the sentences to indicate their correct order.

Item 5

_____ (A) If the coin begins to slow down in the runway, it is deemed authentic, and the customer receives the product.

_____ (B) Vending machines around the world operate on the same basic principles.

_____ (C) Once inside the machine, coins fall into a cradle which weighs them.

_____ (D) The first check is the slot: coins that are bent or too large will not go in the machine.

_____ (E) Coins that pass the weight test then travel down a runway.

Item 6

_____ (A) As one peruses glossy TV magazines nowadays, it is easy to notice how these so-called celebrities seek out the media.

_____ (B) Traditionally, celebrities gained their status by work or achievements in a particular field of expertise.

_____ (C) "Celebrity" is the term used to describe someone who is famous and attracts attention from the general public and the world's media.

_____ (D) For example, the reality TV show Big Brother is everything that George Orwell warned us about: "normal" people are thrust into the limelight to be mocked and humiliated, and we lap it up.

_____ (E) However, as the twenty-first century progresses, a new celebrity has arrived – the nobody.

Instructions: Each of the four following passages in items 7 to 10 contains missing words. Choose the correct word for each gap from the list below each passage.

Item 7

Michelangelo began work on the massive (1) _____ of painting the ceiling of the Sistine Chapel in Italy over six centuries ago. He was assisted by six others who helped to mix his paint and plaster. However, as work proceeded, the artist dismissed each one, (2) _____ that they lacked competence. Described as the lonely genius, the painter himself often felt (3) _____ by the project Yet, he went on to (4) _____ one of the most beautiful works in art history.

claiming / overwhelmed / negative / paint / project / intention / opposing

---

Item 8

Reconstruction is the process whereby (1) _____ are constructed in an undocumented language by comparing its sound system to that of known related languages. The practice, which is also called internal reconstruction, is based on the postulation that certain sounds have variants in various languages. For instance, the Latin word *pater* and the Gothic word *fadar* show a systematic (2) _____ between the *p* and *f* sounds in these languages. This leads to the (3) _____ that *p* was the earlier variant of the *f* consonant in other related (4) _____, as well as in antediluvian languages and Indo-European forms.

words / languages / conclusions / hypothesis / form / correspondence / note / evidence

---

Item 9

"All knowledge that is (1) _____ human society, rather than the natural world, is historical knowledge, and is therefore reliant (2) _____ judgment and interpretation. This is not to say that facts or data are non-existent, but that facts obtain importance (3) _____ what is made of them in interpretation, for interpretations depend very much on who the interpreter is, (4) _____ which academic discipline he or she works, what his or her purpose is, and (5) _____ what historical period the interpretation takes place" (Excerpt from *Culture and Imperialism* by Edward Said).

below / to / from / in / upon / during / about / above

Item 10

Many people will have heard the old song "Don't Worry, Be Happy" by Bobby McFerrin. But is McFerrin's refrain that everyone can choose to live a (1) _____ life by deciding not to worry an (2) _____ proposition in reality? In fact, living a happy and worry-free life is merely an (3) _____ dream for many because life has many (4) _____ events that are often not of our own choosing.

careful / idealistic / stressful / attainable / joyful / unbalanced / simplistic

Instructions: Each of the five following passages in items 11 to 15 contains missing words. Choose the correct word for each gap from the answer choices provided below each passage.

Item 11

Many students dream of attending college and (1) _____ on an exciting career. However, not every student wants to spend three or four years at college. A two-year program in the community college system is an (2) _____ for these students. Community colleges have an (3) _____ enrollment policy, which means that they consider anyone for admission, regardless of grades or test scores. These colleges are (4) _____ to anyone able to pay the tuition. The flexibility of the programs these institutions offer make them attractive to students fettered with family or work-related responsibilities. The community college system is not without its drawbacks, however. One (5) _____ is accommodation. On-campus housing is often not provided for students living away from home. Another consideration is that these institutions do not offer complete Bachelor of Arts degrees, buy only the (6) _____ two-year Associate of Arts degree.

Gap 1

A. traveling   B. creating   C. embarking   D. launching

Gap 2

A. enhancement   B. ability   C. umbrage   D. option

Gap 3

A. admissible   B. open   C. accepting   D. available

Gap 4

A. accessible   B. dedicated   C. capable   D. natural

Gap 5

A. item   B. area   C. condition   D. disadvantage

Gap 6

A. lesser   B. further   C. extra   D. narrower

Item 12

The world's first public railway carried passengers, even though it was primarily designed to transport coal from inland mines to ports on the North Sea. Unveiled in the nineteenth century, the train had 32 open wagons and carried over 300 people. The steam- (1) _____ engine operated by what was termed the steam-blast technique. The chimney of the locomotive redirected exhaust steam into the engine via a narrow pipe. In this way, the steam created a draft of air which followed after it, (2) _____ more power and speed for the engine. The train had rimmed wheels which ran atop specially- (3) _____ rails that gave the carriages a faster and smoother ride. While the small carriages could hardly have been (4) _____ luxurious, the locomotive could accelerate to 15 miles per hour, a record-breaking speed at that time. Subsequently, the inventor of the locomotive, George Stephenson, revolutionized his steam engine by adding 24 further pipes.

Gap 1

A. arranged   B. powered   C. formed   D. constructed

Gap 2

A. lacking   B. needing   C. creating   D. corresponding

Gap 3

A. designed   B. improved   C. composed   D. driven

Gap 4

A. viewed   B. imagined   C. stated   D. called

Item 13

In December of 1880, a friend who was a veterinary surgeon gave Louis Pasteur two rabid dogs for research purposes. Victims of bites from rabid dogs normally showed no symptoms for three to twelve weeks. By then, however, the patient would be suffering from convulsions and delirium, and it would be too late to administer any (1) _____. So-called treatments at that time consisted of burning the bitten area of skin with red-hot pokers or with carbolic acid. Pasteur devoted himself to discovering a more humane and effective (2) _____ of treatment for the disease. His tests on the rabid dogs confirmed that rabies germs were isolated in the saliva and nervous systems of the animals. After many weeks of tests and experiments, Pasteur cultivated a vaccine. Safe since it is derived from a(n) (3) _____ form of the rabies virus itself, the vaccine is administered before the microorganism is encountered and stimulates the immune system to recognize and fight off any (4) _____ exposure to the organism.

Gap 1

A. redress   B. fix   C. restoration   D. remedy

Gap 2

A. method   B. mechanism   C. way   D. approach

Gap 3

A. unreliable   B. uncertain   C. weakened   D. decrepit

Gap 4

A. mandatory   B. future   C. fundamental   D. available

Item 14

An efficient electron microscope can magnify an object by more than one million times its original size. This innovation has thereby allowed scientists to identify and study the (1) _____ molecules that constitute human life. The electron microscope functions by emitting a stream of electrons from a gun-type instrument, which is similar to the apparatus used in an old-fashioned television tube. The electrons pass through an advanced electronic (2) _____ that is accelerated to millions of volts in certain cases. Before traveling through a vacuum in order to remove oxygen molecules, the electrons are focused into a beam by way of magnetic coils. Invisible to the naked eye, electron beams can nevertheless be projected onto a florescent screen. (3) _____ the screen, the electrons glow and can even be recorded on film. In the transmission electron microscope, which is used to study cells or tissues, the beam passes through a thin slice of the specimen that is being studied. On the other hand, in the scanning electron microscope, which is used for tasks such as (4) _____ bullets and fibers, the beam is reflected. This reflection creates a picture of the specimen line by line.

Gap 1

A. analytical   B. precise   C. ambiguous   D. suitable

Gap 2

A. area   B. operation   C. field   D. distance

Gap 3

A. Striking   B. Colliding   C. Forcing   D. Beating

Gap 4

A. criticizing   B. considering   C. appraising   D. examining

Item 15

Improved weather observation practices seem to have reduced the severity of tornadoes in recent years. However, in many (1) _____ of these weather-related events, they continue to be damaging or even deadly. While many people live in fear of tornadoes and the path of destruction they wreak, very few people actually understand how these weather events occur. Even fewer people understand how to protect themselves and their property if a tornado were to strike. Tornadoes develop as the wind changes direction and the wind speed simultaneously increases. This combination of atmospheric changes is (2) _____ to cause spinning movements in the troposphere, which is the lowest level of the earth's atmosphere. The resulting whirling motion, which sometimes is not even visible to the (3) _____, is compounded when the rotating air column moves to a vertical position. The developing tornado draws in warm air surrounding it at ground level, and its speed begins to increase. As warm air is drawn in, a funnel is (4) _____ from the cloud above it. The resulting funnels thus become pendent from low-pressure areas of storm clouds. When a tornado touches the ground, a strong upward draft, which is called a vortex, is formed. The vortex is a circular, rolling column of wind that reaches speeds of more than 200 miles per hour. As it moves across the landscape, the tornado creates a path of destruction. These twisters have been known to lift heavy objects, such as large animals or cars, and cast them off several miles away.

Gap 1

A. cases   B. incidence   C. conditions   D. situations

Gap 2

A. insured   B. bound   C. limited   D. called

Gap 3

A. participant   B. watcher   C. observer   D. looker

Gap 4

A. produced   B. originated   C. disposed   D. emanated

PTE Listening Practice Test 2

Please see the answer key for sample summaries and answers.

To access the recording for this practice test, open the link entitled "Listening Practice Test 2" at:

pte-listening.examsam.com

All of the appropriate timings are provided in the recording, so you may listen to it continuously without stopping if you would like to simulate actual exam conditions.

Item 1:

You will hear a brief class discussion. Write a 50 to 70-word summary of what you have heard. After the recording finishes, you are allowed 10 minutes to complete your summary.

Item 2:

You will hear a short excerpt from a lecture. Write a 50 to 70-word summary of what you have heard. After the recording finishes, you are allowed 10 minutes to complete your summary.

Item 3:

Listen to the recording and choose the correct answers. More than one answer is correct.

What changes does the manager mention in her talk?

      A. Ahmed has resigned and is leaving soon.
      B. Shakira is going to receive a promotion.
      C. The job will be available only to external applicants.
      D. Five individuals will be offered interviews.
      E. Applications are being accepted for general manager.

Item 4:

Listen to the recording and choose the correct answers. More than one answer is correct.

The purpose of this talk is to:

      A. describe the function of each type of brain waves.
      B. provide research from medical professionals about brain injury.
      C. Illustrate how the cerebral cortex can be damaged.
      D. debate controversies in law regarding brain activity.
      E. discuss why the subject of brain death has become contentious.

Item 5:

Listen to the recording and fill in the missing words in the text below.

When most of us think of deserts, we recall (1) _____ deserts such as the Sahara, which consists of over ten thousand square miles of sand-covered (2) _____. Contrary to the popular belief that deserts are vast, sandy (3) _____, only about one-fifth of the desert area on earth is covered with sand. The largest desert in the world, the Antarctica desert, covers roughly five and a half (4) _____ square miles of land space. The Artic desert is second-largest with a size of 5.4 million square miles of land space. Both of these deserts consist (5) _____ of snow and ice, rather than sand.

Item 6:

Listen to the recording and fill in the missing words in the text below.

Organic farming has become one of the fastest growing trends in (1) _____ recently. Farmers have realized that organic farming is an incredibly cost (2) _____ method because it can potentially be used to control costs, as well as to appeal to higher-priced markets. Apart from these (3) _____ benefits, organic farming also naturally results in positive (4) _____ outcomes for the environment. Organic farming relies on practices that do not harm the environment, and for this reason, chemicals and (5) _____ medicines are prohibited. All kinds of agricultural products can be produced organically, including grains, meat, eggs, and milk. Research has shown that organic produce contains lower levels of both chemicals and (6) _____ than food which is produced using conventional farming methods. Scientists have discovered that organic farms contain more species of plants, birds, and insects due to the fact that the (7) _____ of chemicals from pesticides and fertilizers makes these areas richer habitats for animals.

Item 7:

Select the answer that best relates to the recording. Only one answer is correct.

    A. Seniors enjoy flowers because of their fragrance, while employees would rather not have floral arrangements in the workplace.

    B. Flowers can have a positive impact on almost everyone since they calm and improve the mind. Seniors and employees can both derive advantages from floral arrangements.

    C. Floral arrangements can benefit everyone, especially those with low intellects. Seniors and office staff enjoy their fragrance and natural beauty.

    D. Even though plants and flowers can curb the enthusiasm of employees, seniors and others can benefit from the mental stimulation and mood-lifting properties associated with floral arrangements.

Item 8:

Select the answer that best relates to the recording. Only one answer is correct.

    A. IQ testing is no longer utilized due to the unprecedented rise in the popularity of multiple intelligence testing.

    B. In order to be truly intelligent, a person needs to possess many different skills.

    C. Not all students enjoy classroom learning, so multiple intelligences need to be taken into account.

    D. Multiple intelligence theory, which is based on individuals' visual, linguistic, musical, and physical abilities, is generally favored over IQ testing.

Item 9:

Listen to the recording and choose the correct answer. Only one answer is correct.

What is the main idea of this talk?

    A. Daytona Beach is over-populated, and travel there needs to be much better controlled.

    B. The most recent census of Daytona Beach is probably inaccurate.

    C. Tourists enjoy Daytona Beach because of its attractions, amenities, atmosphere, and accessibility.

    D. The most popular attraction in Daytona Beach is its speedway.

Item 10:

Listen to the recording and choose the correct answer. Only one answer is correct.

What is the speaker mainly attempting to express in his comments?

    A. This student's late arrival to class is causing problems.
    B. Most students have complained about the inconvenience.
    C. Many students are late to class, creating distractions for others.
    D. This student misses the refresher session.

Item 11:

At the end of the recording, a beep has been substituted for the final word or words. Select the correct word or words to replace the beep.

    A. clothing
    B. fare
    C. life

Item 12:

At the end of the recording, a beep has been substituted for the final word or words. Select the correct word or words to replace the beep.

    A. would be supported
    B. might be constructed
    C. could be averted

Item 13:

The text of a recording is provided below. Some of the words in the text do not match the recording. Please identify the words that are different.

Cell differentiation occurs when a cell changes into another type of cell or cells. Cellular differentiation occurs in multiple organisms. Cells differentiate when they change from a zygote into a more complicated cellular system. A zygote is a single-celled eukaryotic cell, formed when reproduced cells unite at fertilization. When cells have fully differentiated, they become specialist. For this reason, cell differentiation is sometimes referred to as cell specialization. After differentiation, specialized cells experience changes in their cytoplasm. Specialized cells also take on unique shapes and the cells can then do one specialized job. These changes in the shapes of specialized cells, as well as the chemical changes, allow the cells to perform their unique jobs within the organism. In this way, cells are altered to perform their special functions to become well suited to the jobs they have to do.

Item 14:

The text of a recording is provided below. Some of the words in the text do not match the recording. Please identify the words that are different.

Beginning on January 1st, all international students will be required to perform in a "buddy" system. This system is designed to help international students improve their English language skills, as well as to help them become accustomed with university practices. While grades are not given under this system, participation in the scheme is a necessary requirement for graduating. Any student who is able to provide sufficient evidence of possessing a certificate in English will be excused from participating in the scheme. This includes students who have passed a recognized English language professional examination. Students who have received Baccalaureate of Arts or Science degrees and are now studying for graduate degrees will also not need to participate.

For items 15 to 17, write down the sentences you hear. You need to write each sentence exactly as it is spoken. Write as much as of each sentence as you possibly can. You will hear each sentence only once.

Item 15:

Item 16:

Item 17:

The lecture texts, correct answers, and suggested responses for all of the items are included in the answer key at the end of the book.

Now open the recording entitled "Speaking Practice Test 3" at:

pte-listening.examsam.com

Follow the instructions on the recording as you attempt the practice test that follows.

Speaking Practice Test 3

Read Aloud

For items 1 to 6, read the text aloud as clearly and as naturally as you can, at a good pace, and with good pronunciation and emphasis.

Item 1:

Static electricity develops when articles acquire an electrical charge by rubbing against one another, such as running a brush through human hair or placing a party balloon against clothing. Making contact in this way transfers electrons between the two items, causing energy to build up. High volumes of energy can sometimes originate in this way, and dangerous electrical sparks can even be formed.

Item 2:

South Africa was settled by the Dutch and the British over three hundred years ago. Its economy experienced huge growth as a result of the discovery of the massive gold and diamond deposits which are characteristics of its geology. The South African economy is also bolstered by its grain and citrus fruit crops, as well as the manufacture of chemicals, vehicles, machinery, clothing, and electronics.

Item 3:

Modern horses are thought to have evolved from two broad wild ancestral types: the heavy forest type and the lighter flat-land type. With a muscular body and slender legs, the quarter horse was developed in order to be able to run a quarter mile with great strength and endurance. This subspecies is normally around five feet in height and is popular with ranchers and others tending to large groups of livestock.

Item 4:

Virtual reality is a computing technique in which a person views an output screen, generally worn as a headset, with all of the participant's movements and sounds recorded by the VR system. Flight simulators for pilots, video conferencing platforms, and computer games all rely upon virtual reality systems.

Item 5:

The Save the Children Fund is the largest international children's charity, founded in the United Kingdom and having the Princess as its president. Working together with other foundations around the world, it is concerned with rescuing children from disaster and the long-term care and welfare of children in need.

Item 6:

Statistics deals with the collection and analysis of numerical data. Statistical analysis of data results in the compilation of information that is useful to the general public, such as the indication of averages for a given population and the potential reasons why there are variances from those averages within the population.

Repeat the Sentence

For items 7 to 16, repeat each sentence exactly as it is recorded. You will hear each sentence only once.

Describe the Image

For items 17 to 22, describe each illustration in detail. You are allowed 25 seconds to study each illustration, and then you will need to speak for 40 seconds on each one to give your response.

Go on to the next page.

Item 17:

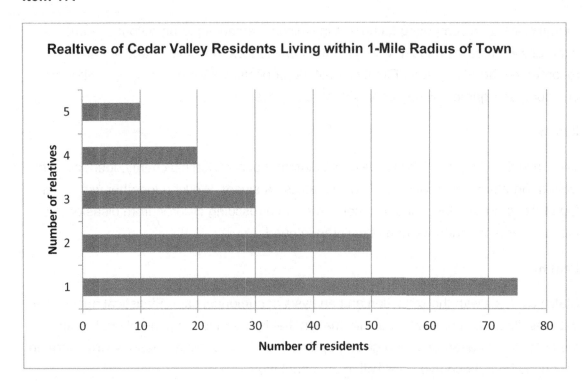

Realtives of Cedar Valley Residents Living within 1-Mile Radius of Town

Item 18:

Electrical Usage by Kilowatt Hours of Eight Houses on Maple Street Last Week

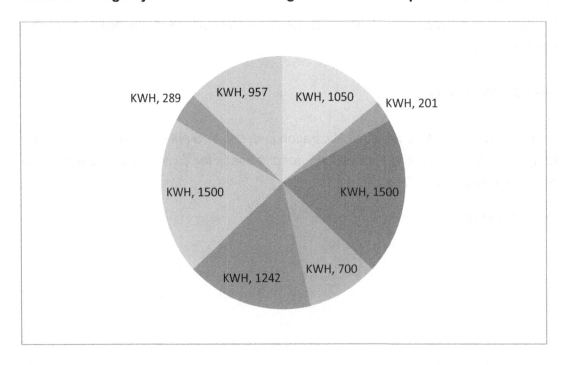

Item 19:

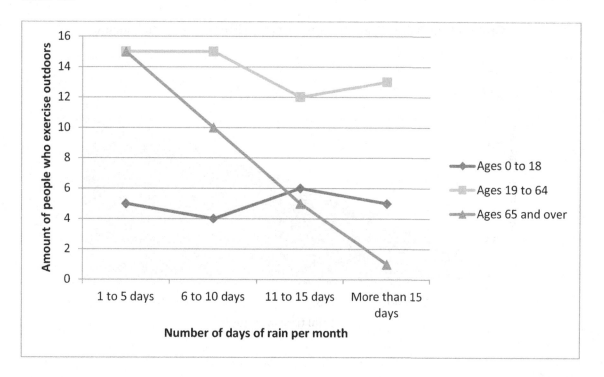

Item 20:

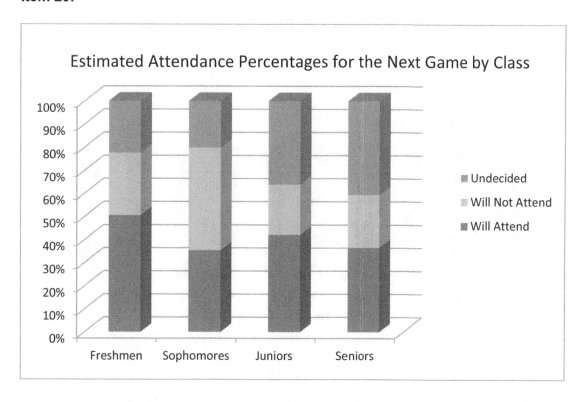

Item 21:

Cumulative Miles Traveled by Aircraft Number 275 Yesterday

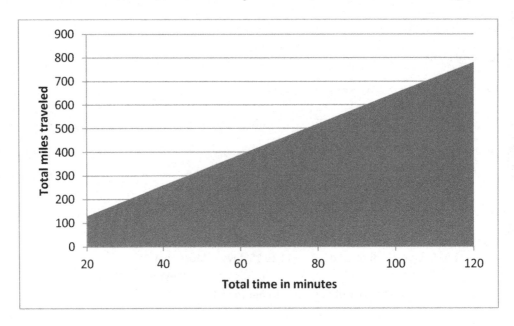

Item 22:

Running Time in Intervals for Race Participant Alex Jones

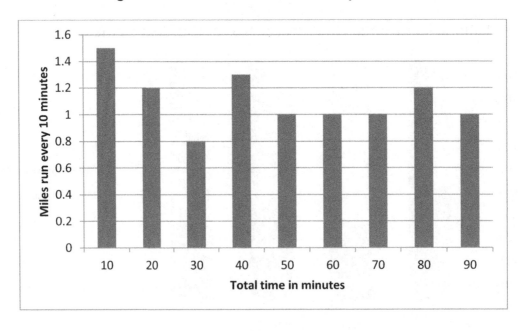

Re-tell Lecture

For items 23 to 25, you will hear talks or lectures. After listening to each one, you will have 10 seconds to review your notes. Then you will be given 40 seconds for each one to restate its contents.

Answer Short Question

For items 26 to 35, you will hear 10 questions. You need to give a brief answer of one or just a few words for each one. For these questions, you should speak immediately after the beep.

PTE Writing Practice Test 3

Instructions: Read the two passages below and write a one-sentence summary of each one. You have ten minutes each to complete these tasks. Each response should contain 75 words or less. When you have finished, compare your responses to the sample summaries on the following pages.

Item 1

Decline rate is a key link in the chain of factors needed to understand the future of the world oil supply. In an effort to answer the question about the increasing rates of decline in oil production, Cambridge Energy Research Associates (CERA) has launched a detailed, in-depth research project. To do the research, CERA undertook a substantive analysis drawing on the most extensive field production database in the world, which includes thousands of fields. Forecasting how much existing oil fields will produce in the future is challenging because the amount that can be produced from a field in any given year varies over time. Production typically rises during a field's early years. This is the build-up phase, which lasts from the onset of production until the field reaches eighty percent of its maximum potential production. After the build-up phase, a field goes into the plateau phase, when it continues to produce at eighty percent or more of its maximum potential. A field then reaches the decline phase, which lasts from the time production first falls below eighty percent of maximum until, after a number of years, production declines to a low enough level that the field is no longer profitable.

Item 2

Clear thinking is crucial for carrying on a conversation, making decisions, and practically everything we do. Thinking can be clouded by a host of conditions including stress, dehydration, and poor nutrition. Now studies reveal that rejection and criticism also have a significant influence on how well a person thinks. In a series of experiments at Case Western Reserve University in Cleveland, Ohio in the United States, participants were exposed to a series of situations that resulted in manufactured rejections. They were given intelligence and analytical-skill tests both before and after the experiment. The researchers were amazed to learn that the intelligence scores plummeted by twenty-five percent on average after the participants had experienced a rejection. Their analytical reasoning skill scores also declined, at an average rate of thirty percent. Since humans are born with the innate fear of abandonment, one of the most powerful drives we have is to connect and be accepted. When rejected, any human being's self-esteem, which is formed in the first seven or eight years of the individual's life, can become unstable. Psychologists believe that self-esteem, which helps build the individual's development of the psychological defenses needed to ward off the slings and arrows of life, is also adversely affected by rejection.

Instructions: Read the essay topics in items 3 and 4 below and write essays about each one. Your responses should be no more than 300 words in length. Give reasons and examples to support your viewpoints.

You are allowed 20 minutes for each essay.

When you have finished, compare your responses to the sample essays on the following pages.

Item 3:

The global industry of tourism is increasingly expanding, but many people fear that this increase in tourism may be causing harm to the local environments in certain destinations.

Is it possible to prevent harm to tourist destinations or should travel to certain countries be curtailed altogether?

Item 4:

In some countries around the world, euthanasia, or the right to die with dignity when terminally ill, is an acceptable practice, but in other countries this practice is not morally acceptable or legal.

Should terminally-ill individuals ever be allowed to end their own lives or is this an ill-advised and dangerous phenomenon?

Item 1 – Sample Response

To assess the reasons why the oil production rate is declining more rapidly than it was previously, Cambridge Energy Research Associates have conducted a comprehensive research project on production in thousands of oil fields around the world, revealing that output in the three discrete phases of build-up, plateau, and decline is extremely variable, and this makes predictions of production very challenging.

Item 2 – Sample Response

Recent research at Case Western University has demonstrated that the important life skills and characteristics of cognitive ability, rational thought, and self-esteem can be notably negatively impacted upon not only by biological but also psychological factors, among which feelings of personal rejection caused by criticism and fear of abandonment play predominant roles.

Item 3 – Sample Essay

Cheaper flights are making it more and more affordable and convenient for people around the world to travel to other countries. In particular, there has been a proliferation in low-cost and budget flights to so-called "exotic" destinations. However, in many cases, "exotic" may mean one of the more remote countries of the world that has not previously suffered from the deleterious effects of tourism. This essay will argue that it is indeed possible to abate the problems associated with international travel through "responsible" forms of tourism.

Because the increase in air travel should give us reason to reconsider our vacation plans, two trends have emerged in the travel industry to deal with the problems associated with expanding global tourism: ecotoursim and voluntourism. Ecotourism, which is aimed at protecting threatened natural environments and intended to support conservation efforts within a host country, is one form of "responsible" tourism. Eco-travelers strive to protect the environment and also develop financial benefits and promote human rights for the local inhabitants of the countries to which they travel.

Promoting the rights of and responsibilities to local inhabitants is also the goal of voluntourism. Traveling in this way involves working as a volunteer in a host country, usually under the auspices of a sponsoring charitable organization. This type of tourism brings benefits to both the traveler and local inhabitants since it allows the tourist to have an adventure, while helping the host country with local issues.

The problems caused by tourism mean that one should devote careful awareness to the effects of a proposed trip on the host country. All in all, it might appear that voluntourism and ecotourism will become even more popular in the future as travelers take the issues of the host country into account when deciding where to go on vacation. [296 words]

Item 4 – Sample Essay

Modern advancements in medicine mean that life expectancy is much longer now than in the past. Yet, in some cases, the life that a seriously ill person lives is full of pain and suffering. The choice about refusing medical treatment to hasten death is one that can be answered competently only if we first respond to two other questions: Who should decide what the best course of action is in each individual case and when?

Clearly, each person has a very different threshold for and tolerance of pain. Patients who have been diagnosed with terminal, incurable illnesses and have been given months to live might prefer not to live during those remaining months if there is going to be a great deal of intense suffering. In essence, the question revolves around the quality of the patient's remaining life.

This question is keenly perceived when the patient shows no brain activity and is being kept alive on a life support machine. The problem is that family members are now placed in the unenviable position of having to make an agonizing choice about ending life support. They may ask themselves what their loved one would have wanted, but in the end, family members ultimately may live to regret their decision.

Several countries are now recognizing Advance Health Directives, in which a person stipulates the conditions for receipt of medical care in the event of personal incapacity. This removes the need for family members to ponder the wishes of the patient since the patient has already committed his or her wishes to writing in advance of any potential illness.

The debate about euthanasia *per se* might continue in cases where the patient has not expressed his or her wishes beforehand. However, Advance Health Directives are certainly a positive step in addressing the issue. [300 words]

PTE Reading Practice Test 3

You are allowed 40 minutes for the reading test. When you have finished, compare your answers to those in the answer key.

Instructions: For items 1 and 2, read the passage and choose the correct answer. *Only one* response is correct for each question.

Item 1

Painted by the Norwegian artist Edvard Munch, *The Scream* depicts the skeletal face of a person in clear psychological distress. Contrasted against a serene background of asymmetrical red and yellow swirls that represent the sunset, the desperation in the facial characteristics of the subject is said to express humanity's reaction to the anxieties of modern life. Completing the work at the age of 29, Munch admitted that he felt as if a scream went through himself during that time since he was in a state of poor mental and physical health while painting the piece.

1.   According to the passage, which one of the following factors most influenced Munch's painting of *The Scream*?
       A. his age at the time of working on the painting
       B. his own lack of psychological and physiological well-being
       C. humanity's experiences of the anxieties of modern life
       D. the asymmetry of his artistic technique

Go on to the next page.

Item 2

Depicting the events of a single day, James Joyce's epic novel *Ulysses* took more than 20,000 hours, or a total of eight years, to write. Set in Dublin, the novel was initially published in installments as a series before a Parisian publishing house issued a limited edition of 1,000 copies. The book was risqué for its time, and was classified as obscene material in the United Stated. After the work was cleared of obscenity charges, an unexpurgated version was accepted for publication by Random House in New York. Ironically, it was not available in Dublin until forty years later.

2.   Which of the following statements is true according to the passage?
    A.   Irish publishers engaged in dilatory practices when dealing with their authors.
    B.   Irish publishers were dissuaded in publishing the novel since it depicted the events of only one day.
    C.   Random House did not have a division in Dublin at that time.
    D.   Publishing guidelines in Dublin were much stricter than those of the United States at that time.

Instructions: For items 3 and 4, read the passage and choose the correct answer. *More than one* response is correct for each question.

Item 3

This line of inquiry is wholly improper and argumentative. It is not a statement as to what the issues are. The judge has already held that this act is constitutional, it being the law of the land. However, there is only one issue before this court and jury, and that is, whether the defendant violated the statute. The jury should be advised that some of the witnesses in this case may have been prejudiced. Furthermore, we have just agreed among ourselves to disregard the so-called evidence and argue the case. (Adapted from the *State v. Scopes Trial*, Delivered by Ben G. McKenzie)

3.   Which of the following most accurately state the opinions of the speaker in the above passage?
    A. The speaker thinks that the judge's decision is incorrect.
    B. The speaker is concerned about the validity of the law.
    C. The speaker believes that the witnesses may not have been unbiased.
    D. The speaker assumes that the proceedings are unconstitutional.
    E. The speaker thinks that the evidence should not be considered.

Item 4

A complex series of interactive patterns govern nearly everything the human body does. We eat to a rhythm, and drink, sleep, and even breathe to separate ones. Research shows that the human body clock is affected by three main rhythmic cycles: the rhythm at which the earth revolves on its axis, the monthly revolution of the moon around the earth, and the annual revolution of the earth around the sun. These rhythms create a sense of time that is both physiological as well as mental. Humans feel hungry about every four hours, sleep about eight hours in every 24-hour period, and dream in cycles of approximately ninety minutes each.

These natural rhythms, sometimes called circadian rhythms, are partially controlled by the hypothalamus in the brain. Circadian rhythms apply to the "lark vs. owl" hypothesis. Larks are those who prefer to rise early in the morning and go to bed early, while owls are those who feel at their best at night. These cycles explain the phenomenon of jet lag, when the individual's body clock is out of step with the actual clock time in his or her new location in the world. In humans, births and deaths also follow predictable cycles, with most births and deaths occurring between midnight and 6:00 am.

4. Which of the following statements can be supported by the above passage?
   A. Most deaths occur according to predictable patterns.
   B. Many people stay up far too late in the evening.
   C. Human behavior is controlled to some extent by particular rhythms.
   D. Some people may have problems with the hypothalamuses in their brains.
   E. Medicine can be taken to deal with jet lag.

Instructions: The sentences in item 5 and item 6 below are in a random order. Number the sentences in each item to indicate their correct order.

Item 5

_____ (A) The ruler did not follow draconian forms of retribution, but rather stipulated that perpetrators of violent crimes pay monetary damages to their victims in lieu of other forms of punishment.

_____ (B) Perhaps best viewed as a way to express personal vengeance, Babylonian punishments included cutting off the fingers of boys who had hit their fathers or gouging out the eyes of those who had blinded another person.

_____ (C) The ancient legal code of Babylonia had severe sanctions for a wide range of crimes.

_____ (D) As with most ancient peoples, the Babylonians did not believe in humane treatments for offenders.

_____ (E) In contrast, Sumerian King Ur Nammu, who formulated a set of laws that were surprisingly modern in their approach.

Item 6

_____ (A) Although many would like to believe that credit card companies are culpable for these high balances, individuals themselves are the real culprits.

_____ (B) Credit card debt is a major cause of over one million bankruptcies each year, but the reason this happens is because many people get a credit card on impulse and fail understand the related fees.

_____ (C) However, with enough willpower and strength to manage finances and spending, consumers can be the winners in the game of finance.

_____ (D) By the time these fees are accrued, payments can be missed, which causes credit card balances to skyrocket.

_____ (E) In short, when credit card debt is out of control, the real cause of the financial mess is the consumer.

Instructions: Each of the four following passages in items 7 to 10 contains missing words. Choose the correct word for each gap from the list below each passage.

Item 7

Educational psychology studies pupils in a classroom (1) _____ in order to help educators understand the behaviors and attitudes that affect learning and teaching. This branch of psychology was a reaction against the psychometric movement, which tested students in order to group them into "streamed" classes of (2) _____ levels of ability. The popularity of "streamed" education declined in the second half of the twentieth century, and the (3) _____ profession is now focused on developing programs that view students as individuals and (4) _____ schools how better to function as organizations.

learning / setting / advising / educational / different / advocating / didactic

---

Item 8

The pyramids at Giza in Egypt were built using only the most (1) _____ tools. Copper saws were used to cut stones, while wooden mallets were used to drive flint wedges into rocks in order to split them. After (2) _____ that the stones were even on all surfaces, wooden rods were joined by strips of twine to check that the stone blocks were completely (3) _____ across the top.

helping / primitive / ensuring / level / advanced / elevated

Item 9

Sir Isaac Newton had the prescience to understand that the (1) _____ study of natural phenomena was of great importance for the scientific community and for society as a whole. It is because of Newton's work that we currently understand the effect of gravity on the earth as a (2) _____ system. As a result of Newton's investigation into the subject of gravity, we know today that (3) _____ features such as mountains and canyons can cause variances in gravity. Newton must also be acknowledged for the realization that (4) _____ force becomes less robust as the distance from the equator diminishes, due to the rotation of the earth, as well as the declining mass and density of the planet from the equator to the poles.

global / weak / geological / gravitational / objective / enigmatic / heavy

Item 10

The use of computers in the stock market helps to control national and international (1) _____. These controls were originally designed in order to create long-term monetary (2) _____ and protect shareholders from catastrophic losses. Yet, the high level of (3) _____ now involved in buying and selling shares means that computer-to-computer trading could result in a (4) _____ in the stock market. Such a slump in the market, if not properly regulated, could bring about a computer-led stock market crash. For this reason, (5) _____ have been put in place by marketplaces such as NASDAQ, ASX, and FTSE.

downturn / stability / regulations / finance / market / automation / computers / downsize

Instructions: Each of the following passages in items 11 to 15 contains missing words. Choose the correct word for each gap from the answer choices provided below each passage.

Item 11

Studies of the human body show that performance ability can be enhanced by regular (1) _____ training exercises. Some human athletic records may seem unbeatable, but these (2) _____ require great effort. When compared to the innate abilities of animals, the athletic training and performance of human beings seem unimpressive, paling in (3) _____ to the phenomenal feats performed naturally by members of the animal kingdom. Whales, for example, usually dive to 3,700 feet below sea level. However, the human body can withstand underwater (4) _____ up to only 2,300 feet, and even attempting to (5) _____ so would require special equipment. Human performance also seems paltry in swimming when contrasted to other species. The human record for the fastest swimming speed is 5.3 miles per hour. However, the sailfish averages a speed of 68 miles per hour, and the penguin, which is not (6) _____ a member of the fish species, can flutter across the surface of the water as fast as 22 miles per hour.

Gap 1
A. forthright   B. formidable   C. strenuous   D. immense

Gap 2
A. achievements   B. behaviors   C. fulfillments   D. administrations

Gap 3
A. analogy   B. comparison   C. connection   D. resemblance

Gap 4
A. bottom   B. expanse   C. extent   D. depths

Gap 5
A. make   B. prepare   C. do   D. accomplish

Gap 6
A. now   B. even   C. regarded   D. heeded

Item 12

In his book *Il Milione*, known in English as *The Travels of Marco Polo*, the intrepid explorer describes the marvels he encountered while (1) _____ to China. Upon his visit to the emperor Kublai Khan in Cathay, Polo witnessed the magical illusions performed by the court wizards of the supreme ruler. Watching in amazement as the wizards (2) _____ incantations, Polo first saw a row of golden cups levitate over the table as Khan drank from each one without spilling a drop. Polo also recounted that Khan had astonishing powers over wild animals. Unrestrained and ostensibly (3) _____, lions would appear to lie down in humility in front of the emperor. Although some academics have disputed the veracity of Polo's written account of the Khan Empire, common sense tells us that there would have been little motive for these events to have been (4) _____ since Polo was being held captive at the time with no hope of release.

Gap 1
A. journeying   B. exploring   C. routing   D. progressing

Gap 2
A. encountered   B. recalled   C. claimed   D. recited

Gap 3
A. taciturn   B. amenable   C. obedient   D. intractable

Gap 4
A. emphasized   B. exaggerated   C. amplified   D. overestimated

Item 13

Recent studies show that coffee may be even worse for us than previous (1) _____ has indicated. We have known for a few years now that coffee can elevate blood pressure and also lead to high cholesterol, but new research has revealed a whole host of other health problems caused by the (2) _____ . For those who frequently suffer from stomach ache, it would be a good idea to cut down on coffee or stop drinking it altogether. A new study demonstrates that coffee stimulates the secretion of gastric acid, which can lead to stomach upset. Consuming coffee later in the day is strongly linked to insomnia, which can cause more health problems like anxiety and depression. Caffeine stays in the (3) _____ system for six hours, so coffee should not be consumed after 2:00 pm unless it is decaffeinated. A further study has shown that coffee changes our sense of taste, making sugary things seem less sweet. This may cause cravings for more sweets. However, one should avoid adding sugar, cream, or milk to coffee. With (4) _____ calorie levels, continued consumption of such fattening beverages can lead to obesity and type-two diabetes.

Gap 1
A. research   B. inquest   C. objective   D. prosecution

Gap 2
A. liquid   B. element   C. beverage   D. item

Gap 3
A. body   B. blood   C. anatomy   D. person

Gap 4
A. promoted   B. developed   C. incremented   D. raised

Item 14

Known as the Centennial State of the United States, Colorado is (1) _____ into sixty-three counties. The eastern part of the state was gained by the U.S. in 1803 as part of the Louisiana Purchase, while the western part was acquired from Mexico by treaty in 1848. Colorado joined the union as the 38th state in 1876, shortly after the first (2) _____ discovery of gold in the state near Pikes Peak in 1859. The Rocky Mountains run along a north-south line through the center of the state, and there are several famous national parks and monuments, including Rocky Mountain National Park, Black Canyon of the Gunnison National Park, Mesa Verde, Dinosaur National Monument, and the Great Sand Dunes National Monument. Agriculture in the state involves the production of wheat, hay, corn, sugar beets, and other crops, as well as cattle ranching and raising other livestock. The (3) _____, processing, fabrication, and defense industries form the lion's share of revenues from business and commerce in the state. Perhaps lesser-known is the fact that Colorado contains the world's largest (4) _____ of molybdenum, a brittle silver-grey metallic chemical element that is used in some alloy steels.

Gap 1
A. detached   B. segregated   C. severed   D. divided

Gap 2
A. hefty   B. strong   C. substantial   D. durable

Gap 3
A. packaging   B. bundling   C. gathering   D. collecting

Gap 4
A. stash   B. deposit   C. savings   D. investment

Item 15

Flowers and bees share a symbiotic relationship since bees benefit from flowers, and flowers could not (1) _____ without bees. Most people know that flowers provide bees with the food that the insects need in order to survive. Bees consume the pollen in the flower, as well as the nectar, the sweet liquid substance that flowers produce to attract the bees. Most bees are social insects that live in colonies of between 10,000 and 60,000 inhabitants. After they collect nectar and pollen from flowers, they fly back to these colonies. They use the nectar to create honey, which then can feed the entire colony. On the other hand, bees also bring (2) _____ to flowering plants, helping the plants to pollinate and therefore reproduce. Plants cannot seek out mates to create offspring in the same way that animals do. Flowers need to have agents, like bees, birds, and even the wind, to move their genetic material from one plant to another. Flowering plants have the male part of their genes in their pollen, and when bees fly from flower to flower, they (3) _____ and deposit this pollen in other plants in the same species. In this way, flowering plants are able to create seeds and reproduce. Without bees, pollination and reproduction would be impossible for most of our plant species, so the work of bees is essential to the ecosystems they in which they live. This means that we can also enjoy various types of fruits, vegetables, and other plant (4) _____ that would not be available otherwise.

Gap 1
A. rise   B. become   C. flourish   D. produce

Gap 2
A. amelioration   B. benefits   C. relief   D. promotion

Gap 3
A. carry   B. pack   C. load   D. bring

Gap 4
A. outputs   B. artifacts   C. aspects   D. products

PTE Listening Practice Test 3

Please see the answer key for sample summaries and answers.

To access the recording for this practice test, open the link entitled "Listening Practice Test 3" at:

pte-listening.examsam.com

All of the appropriate timings are provided in the recording, so you may listen to it continuously without stopping if you would like to simulate actual exam conditions.

Item 1:

You will hear a brief class discussion. Write a 50 to 70-word summary of what you have heard. After the recording finishes, you are allowed 10 minutes to complete your summary.

Item 2:

You will hear a short excerpt from a lecture. Write a 50 to 70-word summary of what you have heard. After the recording finishes, you are allowed 10 minutes to complete your summary.

Item 3:

Listen to the recording and choose the correct answers. More than one answer is correct.

According to the lecture, why do populations sometimes not increase in size?

      A. Families decide that they do not want to have children.
      B. People decide to rebel against governmental policies.
      C. The age-sex structure becomes balanced.
      D. The number of children being born diminishes.
      E. The death rate of the population declines.

Item 4:

Listen to the recording and choose the correct answers. More than one answer is correct.

The purpose of this talk is to:

      A. demonstrate the importance of research carried out in Antarctica.
      B. elucidate the role Antarctica plays in the global ecosphere.
      C. explain why the climate of Antarctica is favorable for winter activities.
      D. lament climate change in Antarctica and around the world.
      E. make an appeal for more research into the melting of the ice sheet.

Item 5:

Listen to the recording and fill in the missing words in the text below.

As we all know, the genetic characteristics of any (1) _____ are present in its DNA. So, DNA is the genetic (2) _____ found in each and every living cell. These form a genetic code and are formed from long (3) _____ like chains, and these DNA chains consist of four separate (4) _____ called nucleotides. Okay, that's a bit of a difficult term. I'd better put that one on the board: "nucleotides." It's the order of these nucleotides on the DNA chain that determines the (5) _____ information for the cells.

Item 6:

Listen to the recording and fill in the missing words in the text below.

I can't reveal any information about what's going to be covered on the end-of-(1) _____ test, but I can tell you that it is a comprehensive test. When a student has a (2) _____ condition, it is considered to be an (3) _____ circumstance, so we can excuse your absence. We will also have to give you more (4) _____ about your homework and so on. As I said, I really can't give (5) _____ details about the final exam, but I would emphasize again that it's a comprehensive test. So, anything we have talked about in class can be included on the final exam. There was a 300-word personal (6) _____ piece that's due next Tuesday, but if you can give me a note from your doctor as (7) _____ , I can give you a two-week extension. Now, here are copies of the PowerPoint slides. Is there anything else I can help you with?

Item 7:

Select the answer that best relates to the recording. Only one answer is correct.

    A. The bilingual approach is generally preferred over the proper names approach when deciphering an unknown language.
    B. While scholars usually know the names of rulers in unknown languages, discovering the meanings of other words is more difficult.
    C. Researchers have two ways to decode unknown languages. The first is by comparing texts and the second is examining proper nouns.
    D. The bilingual approach is often used alongside the proper names approach when understanding the secrets of an unknown language.

Item 8:

Select the answer that best relates to the recording. Only one answer is correct.

    A. Bicycle deaths have increased recently, so safety while cycling is paramount. Before using a bicycle, a person should adjust the seat, wear a properly-fitted helmet, and utilize other biking safety accessories.
    B. Cyclists sometimes fail to protect themselves while riding, which can be fatal. Seat adjustment, mirrors, bells, reflectors, headlights, and helmets are now required by law.
    C. Many cyclists unwittingly face road hazards each year, especially in heavy automobile traffic and road congestion. Accordingly, cyclists should protect themselves with helmets.
    D. Bicycles should not be operated after dark unless a headlight is used. This will help to reduce cycling fatalities.

Item 9:

Listen to the recording and choose the correct answer. Only one answer is correct.

What is the speaker mainly attempting to express in his comments?

    A. Structures that have components made internationally are superior to those built with local materials.
    B. Prefabrication refers to the process of pre-building parts of a structure away from the construction site.
    C. Austria, the United States, Japan, and Germany are leaders in prefabricated building components.
    D. The use of prefabricated components can be efficacious when constructing urban structures.

Item 10:

Listen to the recording and choose the correct answer. Only one answer is correct.

What is the main idea of this lecture?

      A. The importance of meiosis and cell division within human physiology.
      B. Meiosis and the process by which chromosomes separate.
      C. The way that daughter cells differ to each other.
      D. The precise differences between various parent cells.

Item 11:

At the end of the recording, a beep has been substituted for the final word or words. Select the correct word or words to replace the beep.

      A. for chemical increases
      B. to preserve food
      C. to have a natural body shape
      D. for heathy bodily function

Item 12:

At the end of the recording, a beep has been substituted for the final word or words. Select the correct word or words to replace the beep.

      A. this situation
      B. their guard
      C. the break-in

Item 13:

The text of a recording is provided below. Some of the words in the text do not match the recording. Please identify the words that are different.

This lecture provides examples of differentiated cells in palisades and animals, as well as details about their size and functions. Palisade cells are found on the top side of the leaves of plants. Full of chloroplasts, which help with the procedure of photosynthesis, root hair cells in plants are long and thick. They increase the surface area of the top of the plant, helping with the adaptation of water and minerals. As far as animal cells, ciliated cells are small hair-like structures that are found in the evaporatory system. They help to filter the air and to move mucus. Nerve cells are made up of long fibers. Charges travel along the fibers to the brain.

Item 14:

The text of a recording is provided below. Some of the words in the text do not match the recording. Please identify the words that are different.

The tradition of music in the eastern world – in other words, music as we know it today – originated in the genre of chanting. Prior to the thirteenth century, chant was the dominant style of music. Notably, chanting was a monophonic form of music. Now, "monophonic," let's have a look at that word. "Mono" is from a Greek word. It means one thing alone or by itself. "Phonic" is also Greek in originality, and it means sound. So, monophonic music consists of only one sound or vocal that is combined in various notes in a series. Polyphonic music appeared in the sixteenth century, during the Renaissance period. In contrast to monophonic music, polyphonic music composes of more than one voice or instrument, and it combines the notes from the different sources together simultaneously. As polyphony developed, musical traditions began to change, and this meant that music began to rely on a greater quality of voices.

For items 15 to 17, write down the sentences you hear. You need to write each sentence exactly as it is spoken. Write as much as of each sentence as you possibly can. You will hear each sentence only once.

Item 15:

Item 16:

Item 17:

LISTENING SCRIPTS

PTE Practice Listening Test 1

Item 1

Professor: In order to measure brain activity and function, there are various types of equipment, which can perform various types of tests. For instance, we have traditionally used CAT and PET scans for this purpose. Okay, can anybody elucidate . . . between CAT and PET scans?

Student: I'll take a stab at it. If I recall correctly, the PET scan works by means of an inert radioactive substance given to a patient, and this allows the doctor to observe the movement of the substance through the brain. As far as the CAT scan, well, they are like an X-ray of the brain, which is then displayed on a computer screen.

Professor: Yes, that right. Now, can anybody talk about the differences between the appearances of CAT and PET scans?

Student: Oh, yeah. Sorry, I should have talked about that, too. The PET scan shows up as one image, and that image will have different colors, and each one of the colors displays the pattern of the brain activity. With the CAT scan, that's a cross-section, so, unlike the PET scan, it can be viewed from different angles or positions, and of course, as far as patients are concerned, the CAT is far less invasive because they don't need to ingest a radioactive substance.

Professor: Great! In addition to CAT and PET scans, we now have an MRI scan, which as you know works according to the principles of magnetism.

Item 2

Socio-economic status plays a key role in a child's success later in life, rather than intellectual ability, according to a recent study. As an example, let's direct our attention to two elementary school students named Paul and John. Both children are attentive and respectful to their teachers, and both earn good grades. However, Paul's father is an affluent property magnate, while John's dad works on an assembly line in a factory. Even though their academic aptitudes are similar, Paul is 30 times more likely than John to have a high-paying career before reaching his fortieth birthday, simply due to the differences in the economic situations of their parents. Indeed, statistics reveal that students like John have a 12% chance of finding and keeping jobs that earn only median-level incomes. Research dealing with the economics of inequality among adults supports these findings. Importantly, these studies also reveal that the economics of inequality is a trend that has become more and more pronounced in recent years. For instance, in 1960, the mean after-tax pay for a corporate executive was more than 12 times that of the average factory worker. In 1974, the average CEO's pay had increased to nearly 35 times that of the typical blue-collar worker. By 1980, the situation was even worse: the executive's wages and benefits were nearly 42 times that of the average wage of a factory worker. In the twenty-first century, this situation has reached a level which some economists have called hyper-inequality. That is, it is now common for the salary of the average executive to be more than 100 times that of the average factory employee. In fact, in the current year, most CEO's are making, on average, 530 times more than blue-collar employees.

Item 3

The eighteenth century was marked by the development of baroque music. Stringed instruments, particularly the violin, were predominant throughout this epoch. Since many of the German-born composers studied abroad, baroque music was regarded to possess an international style. Other forms of classical music, especially the symphony, also developed during this century. Okay, so, eighteenth century music – many people believe this anyway – was dominated by two German-born geniuses: Bach and Handel. These two composers wrote music in almost every genre, including opera and oratorio music. Handel, of course, studied in both Italy and England, bearing out the point I made earlier about the international flavor of the musical compositions of this century. Bach, while similar in many ways to Handel, is perhaps best known for his liturgical – and by this I mean religious – music. Some music history scholars point out that Bach's work is significant historically, too, since it shows the pervasive impact of the Reformation on the musical style of this century. Finally, then, no lecture on musical genre would be complete without a discussion of Beethoven. Beethoven really was a remarkable and versatile musician. He contributed to almost every style of music during his era, including piano, strings, and symphonies, and he also expanded the form of the symphony to include greater orchestration. Beethoven is often seen as the crucial link between the classical and romantic periods. He added deeper texture – by this I mean the depth and breadth of different types of musical sound – as well as aesthetics – and here by aesthetics we are talking about the beauty of the music itself.

Item 4

Gene splicing . . . this describes the process whereby a small part of the DNA chain for one characteristic of one organism is cut out of the DNA chain for that organism and inserted into the DNA chain of another organism from another species. This has produced results like the "super-tomato." Now, the "super-tomato" was genetically engineered by inserting some DNA from cold-water fish. The particular gene resistance to cold temperatures was isolated on the DNA chain of the fish and was removed. This cold-resistant gene was re-inserted into an ordinary tomato plant, and we've now got tomato plants that can grow in cold weather conditions. Another experiment, that was even more notorious than the "super-tomato," was the . . . Factor 9. Factor 9 is a genetic agent that is responsible for the clotting of blood. Because that person's blood doesn't clot in the normal way, they could suffer extensive blood loss, or even lose their life, very quickly. So, some scientists in Scotland several years ago found a way to grow and extract Factor 9 from sheep and then reinsert that sheep gene into people who were at risk of severe bleeding because they didn't have the Factor 9 gene.

Item 5

The roots of some plants can go extremely deep into the soil. In fact, the roots of some plants extend nearly one hundred feet below ground. However, roots can appear in the most unusual places, including the air. The roots from the banyan tree in southern Asia grow downward from the tree until they reach the ground and anchor into the earth. The banyan tree therefore starts growing as an air plant before its roots grow underground. Conversely, not every part of a plant located below ground is a root. The black locust tree, for instance, sends up sprouts from underground. These sprouts do not come from roots, but rather from underground stems called rhizomes.

Item 6

Group projects at college are sometimes assigned in order to promote teamwork and interpersonal communication skills. When the teacher sets a group project, students are required to work together in small groups in order to achieve the desired outcome. Yet, in my experience, students rarely work together in such an idealistic, cooperative manner. Rather, the one or two responsible students in the group will be left to complete the project, while others shirk their responsibility. I am opposed to the use group projects for assessment purposes since non-motivated students often perform very few of the required tasks and attempt to take credit for the work of the more capable students.

Item 7

A cliché is a commonly-used phrase that expresses a particular idea or sentiment. Most of us use clichés in our day-to-day speech without even realizing it. For example, the phrase "an axe to grind" is believed to come from a popular story by Benjamin Franklin, while the works of Shakespeare have been the source of countless other phrases that have become clichés. Phrases are considered to be clichés when they become overused. Because these phrases so widely over-used, the original sources of many of them have long been forgotten.

Item 8

Earthquakes occur when there is motion in the tectonic plates on the surface of the earth. The crust of the earth contains twelve such tectonic plates, which are from four to ten kilometers in length when located below the sea, although those on land can be from thirty to seventy kilometers long. Fault lines, that is, the places where these plates meet, build up a great deal of pressure because the plates are constantly pressing on each other. So, the two plates will eventually shift or separate because the pressure on them is constantly increasing, and this build-up of energy needs to be released. When the plates shift or separate, we have an occurrence of an earthquake, also known as a seismic event. The point where the earthquake is at is strongest is called the epicenter. In addition, waves of motion travel out from this epicenter, often causing widespread destruction to an area. So, with this likelihood for earthquakes to occur, it is essential that earthquake prediction systems are in place. The purpose of earthquake prediction is to give advanced warning to the population, thereby saving lives in the process. However, these prediction systems need to be reliable in order to be of any practical use. For this reason, scientists are currently attempting to conduct research on the probability of earthquakes along each of the twelve fault lines. Nevertheless, scientists have to exercise care when trying to predict the frequency of future earthquakes based on the number of earthquakes that have happened in the past.

Item 9

I'm living in Henderson Hall right now, but I'm wondering if it will be . . . if I could move to a different residential hall. I mean, I want to move immediately, if possible. It's just that Henderson Hall is quite far from the library. So, I have to carry my laptop and all the books there, and of course, then I have to carry them back to my room again, which is very tiring. It's so distracting in my room with all the loud music. It's really noisy. I can't study in my room, so I am finding it extremely frustrating if I want to read, or write an essay or something. The library has a computer lab, but it's usually completely full, and there aren't any free computers available.

Item 10

Reflex actions are automatic responses within the body to external stimuli. Reflexes are automatic in the sense that they are involuntary, and we don't need to think about doing them. Because we often use them in response to danger or potential injury, reflex actions are rapid responses. The electrical impulses that are responsible for a reflex action travel along a pathway called a reflex arc. Receptors in the body transform stimuli into electrical impulses. These nerve impulses go from the receptor and travel to a sensory neuron. From the sensory neuron, the impulse goes to a relay neuron in the spinal cord. The impulse then goes to a motor neuron. Finally, the impulse leaves the motor neuron and travels to an effector, where the reflex action is carried out.

Item 11

The legend of Robin Hood identifies him as an outlaw figure who robbed from the rich to give to the poor. However, evidence for his existence is flimsy at best. The earliest references to Robin Hood in literature can be traced back to the 13th century. Robin Hood is cited in a British manuscript record for nonpayment of a fine in the year 1225. William Langland mentions Robin Hood in his 14th-century poem entitled *Piers Plowman*. Shakespeare also mentions the outlaw in his play *As You Like It*. In spite of these references, scholars still debate whether Robin Hood was a real person.

Item 12

The term "plastics" includes a wide array of materials that are man-made from carbon and hydrogen. One of the advantages of using plastic as a packaging material is its durability, but the product's durability has also become a problem as plastic cups, bags, and containers are a major source of litter. A possible solution to this problem is biodegradable plastic. Containing starches and chemicals that are easily attacked by light and bacteria, biodegradable plastic gradually breaks into small pieces and is absorbed by the ground.

Item 13

The basement of the building was made waterproof by constructing massive concrete walls, which were built on site section-by-section. Because the ground was so soft, finding the solid bedrock below was an immense undertaking. This was accomplished by utilizing a dredging apparatus to dig a narrow trench. This trench was kept full of heavy clay during its construction to prevent it from caving in. Then, the trench was dug to a depth of thirty-six meters. More trenches were put in place until the site was completely enclosed on its perimeter. Ultimately, the underground concrete wall that functioned as the basement of the building was the height of a twelve-story building. Next, the concrete lower floor of the building was constructed so that work above ground could commence. During the next phase of construction, eight giant steel columns, which weighed more than a thousand tons, were erected to support the walls of the structure.

Item 14

The study of the philosophy of human nature is often regarded as an investigation into the meaning of life. This subject usually deals with four key problem areas: human choice, human thought, human personality, and the unity of the human being. The first problem area, human choice, asks whether human beings can really make decisions that can change their futures. In the second problem area, human thought, epistemology is considered. Epistemology means the study of knowledge; it should not be confused with ontology, the study of being or existence. The third key issue, human personality, takes a look at emotional, spiritual, and communal elements. Importantly, the study of the communal aspect focuses on community and communication, rather than on government or the philosophy of the state. Finally, the fourth problem, the unity of the human being, explores the first three areas more fully and asks whether there is any unifying basis for human choice, thought, and personality.

Item 15: All students need to hand in their assignments on or before next Monday.

Item 16: The Organic Chemistry lecture is cancelled for the 11:00 o'clock session.

Item 17: Marketing students need to write a report on about business planning and funding.

PTE Practice Listening Test 2

Item 1

Professor: Although the trends show that smoking by adults has been declining steadily over the past few decades, the percentage of teenagers who smoke only started to drop in the late 1990's. In fact, the current statistics on this are really quite alarming because, at present, the rate of teenagers who smoke is nearly fifty percent greater than the rate for adult smokers. So, my first question is this: what reasons can you give for these trends?
Student: Well, could it be that teenagers are more prone to pressure from their friends, you know, peer pressure, and so of course they want to fit in with their social group and smoking is one way to do that.
Professor: Yes, good answer. Peer pressure is really one of the biggest reasons why teens smoke. But, you know, peer pressure has always existed from time immemorial. Can you think of any other reasons . . . um . . . I mean reasons that are specifically connected with current social and cultural phenomena?

Student: Oh, yeah, I see what you're getting at. You know, with the increase in the use of things like the internet and with a lot of parents working long hours, maybe kids feel a bit . . . sort of . . . alienated . . . is that the right word? I mean, like if the kid is by himself a lot maybe he's just going to feel alone and not connected to anybody else but his friends and then of course he's more susceptible to fall into the trap of smoking because of peer pressure.

Item 2

Well really, a healthy diet should include food from four major groups. These four groups are carbohydrate, fruit, vegetables, and protein. The first of the four groups, carbohydrate, includes food like potatoes, bread, and cereals. Although carbohydrates seem to have gotten bad press lately, in fact, they are an essential part of healthy nutrition, because . . . well . . . importantly, they provide the building blocks for supplying energy to the body. The second and third food groups are fruit and vegetables – although some people would just include these as one group. This may be easy to understand at first blush, but it is worth pointing out that good nutrition depends on eating a variety of fruit and vegetables. While the old adage "An apple a day keeps the doctor away" may appear to be sound advice, eating the same fruit or vegetables daily . . . um . . . it's not really the best advice in reality. The amount of fruit and vegetables . . . now that's also important to bear in mind. Most medical practitioners now recommend a minimum consumption of five portions of fruit or vegetables every day. Now, protein . . . Protein includes food such as meat and fish, as well as dairy products, like milk and cheese. However, lean protein is better than fatty protein, so it's best to limit the consumption of red meat, rich cheeses, and cream.

Item 3

Okay everybody. Thanks for coming to this special meeting today. Could everyone have a seat please? Okay. Great. Thanks. The reason we're meeting today is to discuss some important changes to the management structure of our company. As some of you already know, Ahmed will be leaving us at the end of this month, so that leaves the position of General Manager open as of the first of next month. We wanted to let you all know that we will be accepting applications from internal applicants from our own company for the next two weeks. This will be followed by interviews for the top five candidates. If – and I should say here, only if – we are unable to fill the General Manager position with a current employee, we will then advertise the job vacancy in the press. If you are interested in applying, you can either fill out the application form online or print one out and send it to Shakira in Human Resources. So, what are we looking for in terms of job requirements? Well, you'll need to have at least five years of managerial experience either here or at another company.

Item 4

There are four types of brain waves. Alpha waves occur in a state of relaxation, while beta waves occur when a person is alert. In addition, delta waves take place during sleep, but they can also occur dysfunctionally when the brain has been severely damaged. Finally, theta waves are of a frequency that is somewhere in between alpha and delta. It seems that the purpose of theta waves is solely to facilitate the combination of the other brain waves. The whole notion of brain waves, then, feeds into the current controversy about death, especially brain death. Of course, this is considered to be very rudimentary, but yet is a very essential question, not only in medicine, but also in law and religion. Some people believe that brain death is characterized by the failure of the cerebral cortex to function. Now, you'll remember that the cerebral cortex is the thinking part of the brain, so under this viewpoint, if a person is no longer physically capable of rational thought, they are considered brain dead. On the other hand, some say that mere damage to the cerebral cortex is not enough. They assert that brain stem function must also cease before a person can be declared dead, because the cerebral cortex is responsible for other bodily processes.

Item 5

When most of us think of deserts, we recall sandy deserts such as the Sahara, which consists of over ten thousand square miles of sand-covered terrain. Contrary to the popular belief that deserts are vast, sandy wastelands, only about one-fifth of the desert area on earth is covered with sand. The largest desert in the world, the Antarctica desert, covers roughly five and a half million square miles of land space. The Artic desert is second-largest with a size of 5.4 million square miles of land space. Both of these deserts consist predominantly of snow and ice, rather than sand.

Item 6

Organic farming has become one of the fastest growing trends in agriculture recently. Farmers have realized that organic farming is an incredibly cost-effective method because it can potentially be used to control costs, as well as to appeal to higher-priced markets. Apart from these monetary benefits, organic farming also naturally results in positive ecological outcomes for the environment. Organic farming relies on practices that do not harm the environment, and for this reason, chemicals and synthetic medicines are prohibited. All kinds of agricultural products can be produced organically, including grains, meat, eggs, and milk. Research has shown that organic produce contains lower levels of both chemicals and bacteria than food which is produced using conventional farming methods. Scientists have discovered that organic farms contain more species of plants, birds, and insects due to the fact that the absence of chemicals from pesticides and fertilizers makes these areas richer habitats for animals.

Item 7

Recent research shows that interaction with flowers and other botanicals has many benefits for our health. In fact, several recent studies link floral products with human well-being. Flower arranging not only combines lovely aromas with beautiful colors and textures, but also makes a person feel closer to nature. In addition, floral design is a creative and calming activity that challenges the mind, requiring its participants to focus on visual skills that improve cognition, information processing, and memory. Another study found that the mere presence of flowers has an immediate effect on mood and happiness. Those in the study who had frequent contact with an environment that had flowers reported more positive moods and less anxiety. Notably, flowers appeared to have the most positive impact upon seniors, reducing depression and encouraging interaction with others. These beautiful plants help employees to have more enthusiasm and energy at work as well, leading to innovative thinking and more original solutions. Studies like these seem to confirm what I have always known instinctively: that having flowers makes us feel better in many ways.

Item 8

Today, we're going to have a look at what's called "multiple intelligences." Now, everybody knows what we mean by IQ, the intelligence quotient. Under this traditional way of measuring intelligence, a person takes an IQ test. But this system has come under criticism recently, because it inheres in many cultural biases. So, there's been a movement away from the IQ test, which basically measures – or at least, is seen as an indication of – a person's academic ability. So, multiple intelligences . . . What do we mean by that? Well, under this new system, intelligence is not just measured theoretically, but practically. For instance, if a person has visual or spatial intelligence, he or she will be good at perceiving visual images and be good at interpreting things like maps and charts and so on. Verbal or linguistic intelligence is another one of the multiple intelligences. Verbal and linguistic ability includes things like . . . if you're good at public speaking or telling stories. There's also musical intelligence, so if you're musically inclined, you probably possess this type of intelligence. Famous sports personalities have what is known as bodily or kinesthetic intelligence. This means that they are skillful in controlling their bodily movements, and of course, they like to keep on the move.

Sitting in a classroom for extended periods of time is definitely not something these types of learners enjoy. Now, Howard Gardner, the researcher who designed the system of multiple intelligence, points out that while most people have one dominant type intelligence, many of us have more than one type. Of course, that's why they're known as multiple intelligences.

Item 9

Daytona Beach is a city located in Volusia County in northeastern Florida. Without taking into account the residents of outlying areas, the city had a population of 61,000 inhabitants in the most recent census. Located approximately 50 miles from Orlando, Daytona Beach is home to various tourist attractions, hotels, and restaurants. These attractions can be accessed by flying into Daytona Beach International Airport, which is situated next to the Daytona International Speedway. Daytona Beach is very popular among college students, who visit it every spring in pursuit of relaxation during spring break.

Item 10

Your persistent tardiness . . . it's become a little disruptive. I mean, I'm sure you've noticed that we usually start the class off with questions and a refresher session from the previous class, so you miss all of that information. It must be inconvenient for you, but you know it's also causing inconvenience in a way to the other students in the 9:00 o'clock class. You have to get another one of the students to repeat all the information to you, and that's where the inconvenience comes in for them, in a way.

Item 11

Although not widespread practice, people have enjoyed eating meals in peculiar places for centuries. Grimond de la Reyniere staged a meal in a Paris mortuary in 1820, where he placed a coffin behind the seat of each guest. In London in the same year, a group of builders regularly had lunch 365 feet above ground, inside a new cross that they were erecting above St. Paul's Cathedral. Louis Sherry had his guests dine on horseback in a dining room of a fine New York City restaurant in 1903. And as recently as last year, a restaurant opened in Latvia, which offers its guests the experience of sleeping in a prison cell and eating prison fare.

Item 12

The HSBC building consists of 47 stories, which is an immense contrast to the twenty-story buildings in its vicinity. In fact, the previous buildings constructed on this site were limited by the soft and often waterlogged ground in the surrounding area. For this reason, the disruption of the ground water supply had to be carefully pondered prior to construction of the HSBC headquarters to ensure that subsidence, and potentially, collapse of the structure, could be averted.

Item 13

Cell differentiation occurs when a cell changes into another type of cell or cells. Cellular differentiation occurs in multicellular organisms. Cells differentiate when they change from a zygote into a more complex cellular system. A zygote is a single-celled eukaryotic cell, formed when reproductive cells unite at fertilization. When cells have fully differentiated, they become specialized. For this reason, cell differentiation is sometimes referred to as cell specialization. After differentiation, specialized cells undergo changes in their cytoplasm. Specialized cells also take on unique shapes and the cells can then do one specialized job. These changes in the shapes of specialized cells, as well as the chemical changes, enable the cells to perform their unique jobs within the organism. In this way, cells are adapted to perform their special functions to become well suited to the jobs they have to do.

Item 14

Beginning on January 1st, all international students will be required to participate in a "buddy" system. This system is designed to help international students improve their English language skills, as well as to help them become acquainted with university practices. While grades are not given under this system, participation in the scheme is a necessary requirement for graduation. Any student who is able to provide satisfactory evidence of possessing a certificate in English will be exempt from participating in the scheme. This includes students who have passed a recognized English language proficiency examination. Students who have received Bachelor of Arts or Science degrees and are now studying for graduate degrees will also not need to participate.

Item 15: For questions about financial aid, you can make an appointment online.

Item 16: The biology exam will take place on the last Thursday of this month.

Item 17: Students must work in groups of three in order to complete the project.

PTE Practice Listening Test 3

Item 1

Speaker 1: As teachers, you'll quickly realize that students are individuals, each operating at different levels of ability. For some students, this might mean that they are operating above the average ability level of their contemporaries, while for others . . . um . . . they may be functioning at a level that is below average. Then, too, there are the students who are in what can be called a comfort zone. These students are learning at the optimum learning level: they are being challenged and learning new things, but yet they don't feel overwhelmed or inundated by the new information. The onus falls on us as teachers not only to work out how best to design the curriculum, but also how to structure classroom learning activities that are going to challenge the maximum amount (sic) of students. The strategy of question adjustment can be deployed to help bridge the gap between those students with low readiness and those with high readiness. Now, who can explain the concept of question adjustment?

Speaker 2: Question adjustment means that the teacher will ask questions at a variety of different levels of difficulty. There will be some so-called easy questions to build the confidence of the students who are less ready. And then, there will also be some really difficult questions, which are supposed to stretch the more capable students, who are the "most ready."

Item 2

Cancer, a group of more than one hundred different types of disease, occurs when cells in the body begin to divide abnormally and continue dividing and forming more cells without control or order. Importantly, all internal organs of the body consist of cells, which normally divide to produce more cells when the body requires them. This is a natural, orderly process that keeps human beings healthy. However, if a cell divides when it is not necessary, a large growth called a tumor can form. These tumors can usually be removed, and in many cases, they do not come back. Unfortunately, in some cases the cancer from the original tumor spreads. The spread of cancer in this way is called metastasis. There are some factors which are known to increase the risk of cancer. Smoking is the largest single cause of death from cancer in the United States. One-third of the deaths from cancer each year are related to smoking, making tobacco use the most preventable cause of death in this country. Choice of food can also be linked to cancer. Research shows that there is a link between high-fat food and certain cancers, and being seriously overweight is also a cancer risk. Cancer risk can therefore be reduced by cutting down on fatty food and eating generous amounts of fruit and vegetables. Skin cancer is the most common type of cancer for both men and women. Repeated exposure to the sun, through sunbathing for example, greatly increases a person's chance of developing this kind of cancer.

Item 3

Certain counties in the world have achieved zero population growth. In addition, some countries have encountered negative population growth, or a net decrease in their population. Now, there are many explanations for these two phenomena. First of all, it's possible that there are low birth rates due to an imbalance in the population's age-sex structure. Low birth rates might also be attributable to governmental policy that attempts to control the population – policies that restrict the number of children a family can have, for example. Another possible reason for these types of demographic changes might be unnaturally high death rates . . . uh . . . in the case of a disease epidemic or a natural disaster. Finally, migration is another factor in demographic attrition, because in any population, a certain amount of people may decide to emigrate, or move to a different country.

Item 4

Antarctica is a mysterious and resilient continent that is often forgotten by virtue of its geographical location. We now know that more than ninety-nine percent of the land is completely covered by snow and ice, making Antarctica the coldest continent on this planet. This inhospitable climate has, not surprisingly, brought about the adaptation of a plethora of plants and biological organisms present on the continent. An investigation into the sedimentary geological formations provides testimony to the process of adaptation. Sediments recovered from the bottom of Antarctic lakes, as well as bacteria discovered in ice, have revealed the history of climate change over the past ten thousand years. Containing nearly seventy percent of the world's freshwater supply, Antarctica plays a crucial role in the world's ecosphere. Therefore, the Antarctic is also a key factor in current global climate change. On its surface, it possesses a four-kilometer-thick ice sheet. This mammoth sheet of ice atrophies because of year-round melting at its base, as well as the loss of ice due to the formation of icebergs. However, the ice sheet is also perpetually replenished by snowfall and frost. At present, two methodologies are employed to measure the size of the ice sheet.

Item 5

As we all know, the genetic character . . . characteristics of any organism are present in its DNA. So DNA is the genetic material found in each and every living cell. These form a genetic code and are formed from long molecules like chains, and these DNA chains consist of four separate components called nucleotides. Okay, that's a bit . . . bit of a difficult term. I'd better put that one on the board: . . . nucleotides. It's the order of these nucleotides on the DNA chain that determines the reproductive information for the cells.

Item 6

I can't reveal any information about what's going to be covered on the end-of-semester test. But I can tell you that it is a comprehensive test. When a student has a medical condition, it is considered to be an extenuating circumstance, so we can excuse your absence. We will also have to give you more leeway about your homework and so on. As I said, I really can't give precise details about the final exam, but anything we have talked about in class can be included on the final exam. There was a 300-word personal response piece that's due next Tuesday, but if you can give me a note from your doctor as evidence, I can give you a two-week extension. Now, here are copies of the PowerPoint slides. Is there anything else I can help you with?

Item 7

When scholars attempt to decipher an unknown language, they have two main methods. The first method is the bilingual approach, in which the unknown text is placed alongside a copy of the text in a known language. The second method is to focus on the use of proper names in a text. Scholars sometimes know the names of kings and other rulers in the unknown language. Therefore, the second method can be effective, even though those who carry out the investigation are not familiar with the majority of the words from the language. Accordingly, scholars usually attempt either the bilingual approach or the proper names approach when trying to unlock the secrets of an unknown language.

Item 8

Bicycling is an excellent way to exercise, see the natural world, and reduce your carbon footprint. However, bicyclists face many hazards, especially when they share the road with vehicles. Injuries can and do happen, even on a designated cycling path. The number of deaths from bicycle incidents increased thirty percent from 2010 to the present. Of these bicyclist deaths, seventy percent involved motor vehicles. There are now approximately eighty million bicyclists on the road with motorized vehicles, so it is of paramount importance that bicyclists take safety precautions to protect themselves. Cyclists would be imprudent not to check their equipment before setting out on any bike ride or journey. The seat should be adjusted and locked in place. It is best to have a rear-view mirror, a horn or bell, and reflectors on the seat, front, pedals, and spokes. When riding after dark, a bright headlight is also recommended. The helmet is often worn incorrectly, thereby offering inadequate protection. It should be adjusted until it fits snugly on the head. Position the sizing pads so that the helmet fits properly. Then place the helmet level on your head, covering the forehead and not tipped backward or forward.

Item 9

First of all, it is interesting to note that a very significant proportion of this structure was prefabricated. In other words, the building was designed so that it had many pre-built parts that were not constructed on site. This prefabrication made the project a truly international effort: the windows were manufactured in Austria, the exterior walls were fabricated in the United States, the toilets and air-conditioning were made in Japan, and many of the other components came from Germany. The prefabrication also had the advantage of making the construction more efficient, as well as minimizing the intrusion and inconvenience to a great many people who continued to work in other buildings near the site.

Item 10

In meiosis, the number of chromosomes in a cell is halved. The daughter cells receive only one chromosome from each pair of chromosomes. So, chromosomes, which occur naturally in pairs, are separated from their other half during meiosis. The essential principal of meiosis is that it consists of two divisions of the cell nucleus, resulting in four cells that contain only one individual chromosome. So, after meiosis is complete, each cell contains only half of the number of chromosomes of the original cell. Meiosis actually consists of two successive divisions. First of all, the parent cell splits in two. During the first meiotic division, the chromosomes line up together. After the chromosomes line up, they separate and go to different cells. During the second meiotic division, the products of the first division split into two again. So, after the second meiotic division, there are a total of four daughter cells. Each of the daughter cells is genetically different.

Item 11

Fresh food is far better than processed food. Packaged food often contains chemicals, such as additives to enhance the color of the food or preservatives that give the food a longer life. These chemicals aren't good for your health for a number of reasons. First of all, they aren't natural and may perhaps be linked to disease in the long term. And in addition, they may block the body's ability to absorb energy and nutrients from food, with nutrients being the essential vitamins and minerals that are required for healthy bodily function.

Item 12

The security guard reported that the burglary was apparently planned. He told the police that a piece of tape had been placed over a lock in a door leading to the headquarters in order to keep the door open. The police also discovered that the men were wearing gloves and that they had filled their pockets with sequentially numbered one-hundred-dollar bills. Most importantly, the men were carrying burglary tools. Even though a ringleader was not named, the police later confirmed that the men were part of a professional ring. The police reported that nothing was stolen, and it was evident that the men had chosen the offices because they were searching for specific documents. It is also known that the men were attempting to repair a bug, which is a secret telephone listening device, that they had installed three weeks before the break-in.

Item 13

This lecture provides examples of differentiated cells in plants and animals, as well as details about their shape and functions. Palisade cells are found on the top side of the leaves of plants. Full of chloroplasts, which help with the process of photosynthesis, root hair cells in plants are long and thin. They increase the surface area of the root of the plant, helping with the absorption of water and minerals. As far as animal cells, ciliated cells are small hair-like structures that are found in the respiratory system. They help to filter the air and to move mucus. Nerve cells are made up of long fibers. Impulses travel along the fibers to the brain.

Item 14

The tradition of music in the western world – in other words, music as we know it today – originated in the genre of chanting. Prior to the thirteenth century, chant was the dominant mode of music. Notably, chanting was a monophonic form of music. Now, monophonic . . . let's have a look at that word. "Mono" is from a Greek word. It means one thing alone or by itself. "Phonic" is also Greek in origin, and it means sound. So, monophonic music consists of only one sound or voice that is combined in various notes in a series. Polyphonic music appeared in the fifteenth century during the early Renaissance period. In contrast to monophonic music, polyphonic music consists of more than one voice or instrument, and it combines the notes from the different sources together simultaneously. As polyphony developed, musical traditions began to change, and this meant that music began to rely on a greater range of voices.

Item 15: Your professor is ill today, so class is cancelled for today and tomorrow.

Item 16: All international students must have an interview to get a degree in English.

Item 17: Any student who copies essays from the internet will receive a mark of zero.

ANSWER KEYS

Speaking Test 1 Answers

You should be able to read each item aloud in under 40 seconds for items 1 to 3 and in under 35 seconds for items 4 to 6. The words with primary emphasis are <u>underlined</u> and the words with secondary emphasis are in *italics*. The items without emphasis are in normal font.

Go to "Read Aloud Examples – Test 1" at pte-listening.examsam.com and repeat each item under timed conditions in order to practice your speed, pronunciation, and emphasis.

Item 1: A *computer system* is called a "<u>turnkey system</u>" when it is purchased from a supplier as an <u>assembled unit</u> in which the *necessary* software is <u>already installed</u> within the required *hardware*. Businesses that <u>prefer</u> turnkey systems <u>do so</u> because there is *usually* no need to perform any <u>system analysis</u> or <u>design</u> exercises on computers acquired in this way.

Item 2: The term "<u>business cycle</u>" refers to the *tendency* for <u>profit-making</u> *activity* within <u>any</u> *country* to *fluctuate* over *time*, rather than experiencing <u>steady growth</u>. Such fluctuations have existed ever since <u>economic</u> record-keeping <u>began</u> and can be caused by factors such as <u>natural catastrophes</u>, *changes in* <u>banking policies,</u> and <u>political upheavals</u>, including *revolution* and *war*.

Item 3: The <u>World Health Organization</u> was established in <u>1948</u> within the *United Nations* in order to <u>promote</u> *international cooperation* in global health issues. The <u>control of diseases</u> is its *primary* concern, but it <u>also</u> assists in <u>vaccinations</u>, <u>water supply</u>, and <u>sanitation</u> around the world. In <u>addition</u>, it is in possession of a <u>great deal</u> of information relating to <u>drug abuse</u>, <u>nuclear hazards</u>, and <u>cancer research</u>.

Item 4: Located in *South America*, <u>Brazil</u> is a low-lying land mass within the <u>Amazon basin</u> on the <u>east side</u> of the *continent*, where the <u>forest canopy</u> *was cleared* in order to create timber reserves. It was settled in the sixteenth century by *Portugal* and has an almost <u>entirely</u> *tropical* climate, with <u>average</u> <u>cumulative</u> <u>annual</u> *rainfalls* of up to 80 inches.

Item 5: The <u>turn-over tax</u> is charged during the *production* process, as *goods* are <u>transformed</u> from <u>raw</u> *materials* to finished products. For *example*, <u>bakeries</u> pay it on *flour*, <u>carpenters</u> pay it on *wood*, and sometimes the <u>customer</u> will even pay it on the *final* *produc*t. Unlike <u>other</u> *taxes*, no credit *is* offered <u>against</u> the *tax* for amounts *previously paid.*

Item 6: The *Canadian* <u>water weed</u> is a *plant* that is native to <u>North</u> *America*. It can grow up to nearly <u>four meters</u> in height and has <u>white flowers</u> with *dark green leaves*. Many years ago, the weed was introduced to <u>Europe</u>, where they are *now* sometimes regarded as a <u>nuisance</u> because they <u>frequently</u> block *waterways*.

Item 7: Post-graduate students will need to learn to teach small groups as a degree requirement.

Item 8: She's already received a Bachelor's degree in Business Studies from another university.

Item 9: Students will need to join the online platform to access the course materials.

Item 10: The conference on language learning will take place in London.

Item 11: Most online businesses earn income by placing advertising on their websites.

Item 12: Shanghai is an important city for international trade and commerce.

Item 13: Scientists are currently attempting to conduct research in order to investigate this issue.

Item 14: The final exam covers all of the topics that we have discussed this semester.

Item 15: We'll have a look at why this topic has become such a troublesome issue recently.

Item 16: There is a bank on the corner, opposite the student union.

Item 17: The line graph shows the percentage amounts of students who failed to complete their university studies. In 1940, the drop-out rate was at its highest on average for all three universities, but it was at its lowest in 2010. While the figures for Universities A and C fell dramatically, the failure-to-complete rate for University B remained more-or-less stable. University A had the highest retention rate, with University C in second place, and University B in third place.

Item 18: The bar graph displays the number children suffering from one or more different diseases in a particular school during a certain year. Around 55 of the children caught only one disease, while approximately 44 children had two diseases during the year.

Thirty of the children had 3 diseases, 20 children had four diseases, and 10 children had 5 diseases during the year. So, the number of children getting multiple ailments constantly declined with each new disease in circulation.

Item 19: The pictogram highlights the amount of positive feedback from customers for four regions during a three-month period. Region 1 had the highest satisfaction rating for the time period with four thousand customers. The lowest level of customer satisfaction was in Region 3, which at 2,000 positive comments was only half that of Region 1. Occupying the middle ground, Regions 2 and 4 had positive ratings from three thousand customers each.

Item 20: The pie chart exhibits the percentages of four different kinds of animals in a zoo at the end of a specific year. The reptile category was the largest group, constituting 42 percent of all of the zoo's creatures. In second place was quadrupeds, with 26 percent of the zoo consisting of these types of animals. Birds and fish had the lowest amounts and were nearly tied for last place, with percentages of 17 percent and 15 percent respectively.

Item 21: The bar chart reveals how many types of accidents with four different kinds of vehicles occurred in Springfield during a four-month period. Cars were involved in the greatest number of accidents overall, with more than twenty-eight accidents each month. June was an especially poor month for van drivers, who experienced twenty accidents this month. With between five and eleven accidents per month, pick-ups and SUV's accounted for the smallest number of collisions.

Item 22: The illustration shows the cash activity during a two-month period for Zarah Company. According to the chart, seventy thousand dollars was received each month in January and February. The cash payments in January were forty thousand, and those in February were higher at sixty thousand. Therefore, the company started the year with one hundred thousand dollars in cash, and two months later, it had increased its cash fund by forty thousand dollars, for a total of one hundred and forty thousand dollars.

Item 23 – Text

Speaker 1: In an article that you wrote recently, you were talking about the laws of physics over the centuries. Can you give us some more background about the development of some of these theories of physics?

Speaker 2: Yes, I sure can. Well, two thousand years ago, a theory developed that a central force moved objects toward the center of the earth. So, this idea of a central force was really very significant.

Speaker 1: Okay, so can you tell us more about what grew out of that theory?

Speaker 2: Many important concepts grew out of that theory, but the first I'll talk about concerns the rate of falling objects. Really, around seven hundred years ago physics started to be studied widely, and it was then discovered that objects with different weights fall to earth at the same speed. So, for instance, a feather and a rock have the same rate when falling to the earth.

Item 23 – Example Response

The speaker starts off by describing the theory of physics whereby a central force within the planet causes objects to move toward the earth's center. This was an important theory because it led to the discovery of another significant concept around seven centuries ago, namely that objects fall to earth at the same rate, regardless of their weights. As an example, a feather and a stone travel at the same rate when falling down to the ground.

Item 24 – Text

Interviewer: In today's seminar, we are going to talk with Professor O'Connell about the qualities of a good teacher. Professor O'Connell, you've been teaching at the university for many years now. Can you recall the name of one your favorite teachers?
Interviewee: My favorite teacher was Mrs. Martinson. She taught me in the third grade when I was only eight years old, and although I was quite young when she was my teacher, she left an indelible impression on me.
Interviewer: What do you remember most about her?
Interviewee: It's been many years since I saw Mrs. Martinson, but the thing I remember most fondly about her was the way that she always encouraged me to do my best.
Interviewer: What do you think made her such a good teacher and role model?
Interviewee: I would sometimes get discouraged, especially during math lessons, but she would never get impatient. She would always come back to my desk where I was working and answer my questions in a very kind way. She taught me at a young age the importance of being kind, and patience to others.

Item 24 – Example Response

The main subject of the talk is which qualities help make a teacher a good one. The professor being interviewed talked about his favorite teacher, who taught him when he was very young, at just eight years of age. The teacher really impressed the speaker because she gave him individual attention when he needed it most. The professor also mentioned that this particular teacher was always encouraging, patient, and kind, and these qualities made her a good teacher and role model.

Item 25 – Text

Fair-trade organizations have created what is known as fair-trade coffee. This is based on a cooperative farming approach, which means that all of the farmers have to work together in order for the system to work. Coffee farmers must pay fees to take part, but in exchange for what they pay, they are guaranteed to receive a price per pound for their harvested coffee beans. Their fees are actually deducted from the amount they earn from the coffee beans, and then a small amount is also deducted for local classes and further education – because, of course, without education about how best to grow their product, the program wouldn't be as successful as it is.

Now, while the whole concept of fair-trade coffee has its supporters, some people actually find fault with the system. The primary complaint seems to be that fair-trade coffee beans are poor quality. But, to understand this complaint about quality, we need to look the different prices that coffee growers can get for their products. The coffee market is divided into different categories based on quality and price, so there are different quality classifications, from the lowest quality, which is called standard grade, to the highest quality, known as specialty grade. It has been discovered that some farmers sell their lower quality coffee as fair-trade, and of course, this causes the quality of the coffee to suffer. Farmers end up selling their higher-grade coffees on the open market, out of the fair-trade system, because they can get a much higher price for it this way. So, sometimes consumers who buy fair-trade beans get a lower-quality product, which may have a poor flavor.

Item 25 – Example Response

The speaker is discussing fair-trade coffee and how farmers work cooperatively in this system. Fees are deducted from the harvest price of the coffee for membership and education about how to grow the product. The biggest complaint about this type of coffee is that a lower-quality, poor-flavored product sometimes ends up with the fair-trade classification. This happens because farmers can get a higher price for their harvest this way, by selling the higher-quality, specialty-grade product on the open market, outside the fair-trade system.

Item 26: How many years are there in a decade? *ten*

Item 27: What is worse: life in prison or a suspended sentence? *life in prison*

Item 28: How many children are there in a set of triplets? *three*

Item 29: What is longer: an inch, a foot, or a mile? *a mile*

Item 30: What type of equipment would most likely be used by a mechanic: sewing machine, tools, or paint brushes? *tools*

Item 31: How many sides are there in a pentagon? *five*

Item 32: Which is usually the safest to drink: sea water, tap water, or bottled water? *bottled water*

Item 33: What is the purpose of an x-ray: to see broken bones or to administer medicine? *to see broken bones*

Item 34: How many years are there in a century? *one hundred*

Item 35: What device can be used to mix food: a drill, a blender, or a chopping board? *a blender*

Reading Test 1

Item 1: B

Item 2: A

Item 3: D and E

Item 4: B and D

Item 5: C, A, E, D, B

Item 6: E, C, A, D. B

Item 7:

(1) complex

(2) similar

(3) rapid

(4) commercial

(5) beautiful

Item 8:

(1) including

(2) members

(3) interpreted

(4) studies

Item 9:

(1) signature

(2) approval

(3) countries

Item 10:

(1) massive

(2) scientific

(3) elusive

(4) greatest

Item 11:

(1) C

(2) B

(3) A

(4) D

(5) C

(6) B

Item 12:

(1) C

(2) A

(3) B

(4) D

Item 13:

(1) C

(2) A

(3) B

(4) D

Item 14:

(1) A

(2) B

(3) C

(4) D

Item 15:

(1) D

(2) B

(3) C

(4) A

Listening Test 1

Item 1 – Sample Summary: CAT, PET, and MRI scans examine brain activity. A radioactive substance is given to the patient for a PET scan, and doctors evaluate the patterns of brain activity by looking at the different colors in the image. A CAT scan is like an X-ray, and it is a cross section of the brain that can be looked at from different angles, while the MRI operates by use of magnetism.

Item 2 – Sample Summary: Socio-economics during childhood is a better indicator of future success than intellect. When compared blue-collar families, children from wealthier backgrounds are thirty times more likely to land high-level jobs by the age of forty. Only twelve percent of children from blue-collar backgrounds will receive even mid-level jobs. Statistics reveal that inequality grew dramatically throughout the twentieth century, and the situation is now so severe that it is called hyper-inequality.

Item 3: The correct answers are B and C.

Item 4: The correct answers are B and D.

Item 5: The roots of some plants can go (1) <u>extremely</u> deep into the soil. In fact, the roots of some plants (2) <u>extend</u> nearly one hundred feet below ground. However, roots can (3) <u>appear</u> in the most unusual places, including the air. The roots from the banyan tree in southern Asia grow (4) <u>downward</u> from the tree until they reach the ground and anchor into the earth. The banyan tree therefore starts (5) <u>growing</u> as an air plant before its roots grow underground. (6) <u>Conversely</u>, not every part of a plant located below ground is a root. The black locust tree, for instance, sends up sprouts from underground. These sprouts do not come from roots, but rather from underground (7) <u>stems</u> called rhizomes.

Item 6: Group projects at college are sometimes assigned in order to promote teamwork and (1) <u>interpersonal</u> communication skills. When the teacher sets a group project, students are required to work together in small groups in order to achieve the (2) <u>desired</u> outcome. Yet, in my experience, students rarely work together in such an idealistic, (3) <u>cooperative</u> manner. Rather, the one or two responsible students in the group will be left to complete the project, while others (4) <u>shirk</u> their responsibility. I am opposed to the use group projects for (5) <u>assessment</u> purposes since non-motivated students often perform very few of the required tasks and attempt to take credit for the work of the more capable students.

Item 7: The correct answer is B.

Item 8: The correct answer is D.

Item 9: The correct answer is C.

Item 10: The correct answer is A. The other answers are specific points form the lecture.

Item 11: The correct answer is B. The purpose of this passage is to discuss Robin Hood's true existence.

Item 12: The correct answer is C. *Biodegradable* means that something can be absorbed into the ground.

Item 13: *For items 13 and 14, the incorrect words are underlined and the correct words have been placed in brackets.*

The basement of the building was made watertight [waterproof] by constructing massive concrete walls, which were built on site section-by-section. Because the ground was so soft, finding the solid land [bedrock] below was an immense undertaking. This was accomplished by utilizing a dredging appliance [apparatus] to dig a narrow trench. This trench was kept full of heavy clay during its construction to prevent it from falling [caving] in. Then, the trench was dug to a depth of thirty-six meters. More trenches were put in place until the site was completely enclosed on its sides [perimeter]. Ultimately, the underground concrete wall that functioned as the basement of the building was the height of a twelve-story building. Next, the concrete upper [lower] floor of the building was constructed so that work above ground could commence. During the next phase of completion [construction], eight giant steel columns, which weighed more than a thousand tons, were erected to support the walls of the structure.

Item 14: The study of the psychology [philosophy] of human nature is often regarded as an investigation into the meaning of life. This subject usually deals with four key problematical [problem] areas: human choice, human thought, human personality, and the unit] of the human being. The first problem area, human choice, asks whether human beings can actually [really] make decisions that can change their futures. In the second problem area, human thought, epistemology is considered. Epistemology means the study of knowledge; it should not be confounded [confused] with ontology, the study of being or existence. The third key issue, human personality, takes a look at emotional, spiritual, and community [communal] elements. Importantly, the study of the communal asset [aspect] focuses on community and communication, rather than on government or the philosophy of the state. Finally, the fourth problem, the unification [unity] of the human being, explores the first three areas more fully and asks <u>when</u> [whether] there is any unifying basis for human choice, thought, and personality.

Item 15: All students need to hand in their assignments on or before next Monday.

Item 16: The Organic Chemistry lecture is cancelled for the 11:00 o'clock session.

Item 17: Marketing students need to write a report about business planning and funding.

Speaking Test 2 Answers

You should be able to read each item aloud in under 40 seconds for items 1 to 3 and in under 35 seconds for items 4 to 6. The words with primary emphasis are <u>underlined</u> and the words with secondary emphasis are in *italics*. The items without emphasis are in normal font.

Go to "Read Aloud Examples – Test 2" at pte-listening.examsam.com and repeat each item under timed conditions in order to practice your speed, pronunciation, and emphasis.

Item 1: There are <u>various</u> estimates of the *number* of <u>countries</u> in the world, depending upon how a <u>country</u> or <u>nation state</u> is *defined*. <u>Most</u> estimates *indicate* that there are nearly <u>200 countries</u> on our planet*, in* <u>addition</u> to the *territories* that claim *independence* through <u>self-declaration</u> or <u>territorial autonomy</u> by having their <u>own leaderships</u>, <u>flags</u>, <u>postage stamps</u>, and *military systems*.

Item 2: <u>First aid</u> is the <u>management</u> and <u>treatment</u> of a *victim* of injury at the *site* of an <u>accident</u> or <u>incident</u>. Whether the patient is <u>conscious</u> *or* <u>unconscious</u>, it is important to *check* for respiration and <u>heartbeat</u>, to *limit* any <u>bleeding</u>, and to *handle* any <u>wounds</u> as <u>gently</u> as possible. <u>Tea</u>, <u>alcohol</u>, <u>coffee</u> or <u>other</u> *fluids* should <u>not</u> *be administered*, nor should <u>any food</u> be provided for *consumption*.

Item 3: The word "<u>investments</u>" in *economics* is chiefly assigned to <u>two different</u> but related enterprises. The <u>first</u> is the acquisition of *assets* in order to *generate* <u>income</u> or <u>other</u> <u>productive</u> <u>gains</u>, such as placing *money* in a <u>bank</u> or *purchasing* <u>stocks</u>, while the <u>second</u> is the *creation* of <u>investments</u> such as <u>equipment</u>, <u>factories</u>, <u>buildings</u>, and <u>other</u> <u>structures</u> or *works in progress*.

Item 4: A <u>black box</u> is a *complete unit* in a <u>computer</u> or electronic system whose <u>internal</u> <u>function</u> need not be understood by the <u>user</u> in order to *operate* it. The term is <u>commonly</u>

used to refer to the <u>data</u> *recorder* in <u>aircraft</u> which collects *information* about the plane's performance during a <u>flight</u> and which can be *utilized* to investigate the <u>cause</u> *of a crash.*

Item 5: There are a <u>number</u> of *schemes* presently in use to <u>divide</u> the <u>Earth</u> into regions by *climate*, based on <u>average</u> *annual temperature*, *mean* <u>monthly</u> *temperature*, and total <u>snow</u> or *rainfall.* Although <u>land position</u> generally determines the amount of *sunshine* any region *receives*, <u>elevation</u> is what most <u>greatly affects</u> *snow and rainfall.*

Item 6: *Natural laws* in <u>science</u> are <u>descriptive</u> *laws* which attempt to explain the behavior of *objects* at <u>rest</u> or in *motion* in the <u>physical world</u>. *However,* within the <u>legal</u> system, *natural law* is said to define how <u>people</u> ought to behave, *and* is rooted in <u>ethics</u>, <u>philosophy</u>, and the <u>observation of human nature</u>.

Item 7: Our university is a world leader in medical research.

Item 8: The library will be open late during final exam week.

Item 9: The professor can see who actually completed the assignment first by looking at the dates.

Item 10: Scientists are working hard to find a cure for the disease.

Item 11: Class is going to start ten minutes late on Wednesday.

Item 12: The professor excluded the non-participating student from the project.

Item 13: Graduate students will need to conduct research in a specific subject area.

Item 14: Financial aid applications are available in the administration building.

Item 15: If you don't work hard, you will never succeed in life.

Item 16: The predictions have to be accurate if they're going to be considered useful.

Item 17: The amounts of production for five products for the month of July are represented in the illustration. The products are listed in ascending order by their product numbers, and this correlates to descending order of the number of units produced. Product 1 had the highest production rate, with an output of five thousand units, while Product 5, at two hundred and fifty units, was the smallest with this minuscule level of production. The other products appear to have moderate levels of output in the thousands.

Item 18: The bar chart exhibits the number of deaths in Jackson county during the previous year for three different diseases and age groups by gender. Cancer caused the most total deaths by far overall for both men and women in all three age groups. HIV led to the lowest death rate for all age groups, with only a fraction of the deaths caused by cancer. Females had lower death rates than males for all age groups and diseases, apart from cancer in the 40-to-59 and 60-and-over age groups.

Item 19: The pie chart reveals how facilities in five different categories are utilized at Northern College. The bar in the student union had the highest usage of any subcategory, and when combined with the meeting rooms in the same facility, the student union had the largest utilization rate overall. The coffee shop and free wi-fi facilities in the cafeteria followed in second place. The other facilities category had the lowest level of usage at only four percent.

Item 20: The line graph displays the five different types of contributions to funds for three different categories of expenditure for New Town library. The greatest amount was by charitable contributions to building costs, which was followed by state and federal contributions to the same costs. The amount of contribution to other expenses constantly appears to be very low, at less than five-hundred dollars for each of the five contributors. Apart from individual and other contributions, operating expenses occupied the middle position overall.

Item 21: The map shows which countries use proprietary exams for placement testing around the world. With 3,000 universities, China had the greatest level of participation in these types of exams, and this was closely followed by Australia and the United States, which appear to have participation levels of around two thousand five hundred universities each. All other countries had much lower levels, besides Mexico and India, which are very conspicuously absent with their lack of participation in such tests.

Item 22: The chart presents the time in minutes for fifteen contestants in a racing event. The winner of first place was contestant number 13, with a time of 9 seconds. The contestants with tag numbers 8 and 12 came in jointly in last place, with times of 23 minutes each, although contestant 9 came in very close to this, with a time of 22 seconds. The other eleven contestants had times ranging from 12 seconds to 21 seconds.

Item 23 – Text

Improving the health of individuals in lesser-developed countries is not merely about providing them with fresh water. A whole host of factors needs to be considered, and an integrated approach is the only sure and predictable way to find a lasting solution to this problem. Communities must first learn the basic principles of hygiene, including important information on how disease spreads and grows. They should also receive education on matters like hand washing, so they should be provided with soaps and detergents, in addition to fresh water. Of course, the problem of human waste disposal must also be evaluated since waste can easily contaminate even the cleanest of water supplies. Finally, the sustainability of the new well of water supply needs to be considered especially carefully. It is of no practical use to provide a supply of water that will not last for at least two decades.

Item 23 – Example Response

The subject of the talk is health and water supply in lesser-developed countries. The speaker explains that the situation is multi-faceted and that hygiene issues are paramount, especially understanding the way that diseases spread, the correct way to hand wash, and how to remove waste properly since water can be contaminated without this. Finally, the water supply needs to be capable of being sustained, and the supply should last for at least twenty years.

Item 24 – Text

Speaker 1: Professor Ahmad is here from the psychology department to discuss personality theory. Professor, could you tell us, in general, roughly how many different types of personalities there are?
Speaker 2: Most psychological theories support the view that there are two broad personality types. This broad classification deals with the way in which we relate to other people and receive our stimulation. The term extrovert is used describe people who prefer to interact with the outside world, including interactions with other people. On the other hand, the function introvert includes those who prefer to receive stimulation from time alone; that is, they are internally-focused individuals.
Speaker 1: Okay, great, that covers the classifications of introvert and extrovert. What kinds of variations are there on these two broad types?
Speaker 2: Some variations on that are the sensing and the intuitive aspects of personality theory. Sensing individuals function by trusting their five senses. In other words, sensing involves perceiving information that is external to the individual. Conversely, the intuitive function means that a person relies on instinct, which is his or

her inner voice, to process information. So, a sensing personality would need to process data and information in order to be comfortable making a decision, although people who are more intuitive would base decisions generally just on how they feel about something within themselves.

Item 24 – Example Response

The professor is describing personality theories, especially the general classifications of introvert and extrovert. She clarifies that introverts are internally-focused and prefer to spend time alone, while extroverts are externally-focused and prefer to interact with other people. She then describes the sensing and intuitive aspects of the personality, in which the sensing type of person likes to base decisions on outside information, although intuitive personality types would rather just listen to their own inner voices.

Item 25 – Text

Okay everybody, I think we should probably get started. In the lecture for today, we're going to take a look at a hotly-debated and contentious topic: genetic engineering. So, first of all, we'll go into a little bit of the background information about this topic, and then we'll move on to consider the nuts and bolts. Okay . . . genetic engineering . . . now as biology students you'll know that this term refers to the process of re-programing the genetic materials that dictate how a plant or animal behaves. And it's probably no surprise to you that scientists have been conducting genetic engineering on plants for quite a few years now . . . things like cereals and fruit, for example. Now, this has been done to produce better fruit . . . to grow fruit or even vegetables, for that matter . . . outside of their normal season, and to make other plants more resistant to damage from insects and disease. So, of course, the next question is . . . well . . . all may be aware of the basic idea behind genetic engineering, but what I'm exactly . . . um . . . I'm referring to is . . . how is genetic engineering carried out on a genetic or biological level specifically and precisely? That's the question we'll look at.

Item 25 – Example Response

The lecture is on the topic of genetic engineering, which is a controversial topic. The speaker explains that genetic engineering is the way that the genetic materials of a plant or animal can be reprogrammed, and cites the improvements in growing cereals, fruit, and vegetables off-season and making them more robust against insect infestations and crop diseases. At the end, he was going to talk about the exact way that genetic engineering is conducted biologically.

Item 26: What part of the body does a podiatrist deal with?   *the feet*

Item 27: How many events are there in a biathlon?   *two*

Item 28: How many years are there in a millennium?   *one thousand*

Item 29: What is the purpose of a respirator?   *to help someone breathe*

Item 30: How many sides are there in an octagon?   *eight*

Item 31: What do we call the alphabetical list of topics placed at the end of a book?   *an index*

Item 32: What is the name of the electrical device that is used to clean the floor?   *vacuum cleaner*

Item 33: Which of the following is used to view objects at a distance, such as watching birds: binoculars or a telescope?   *binoculars*

Item 34: A construction project requires working at height. What is the most appropriate piece of equipment for workers on this site - safety harnesses, ventilators, or cushions?   *safety harnesses*

Item 35: Which medical procedure is the most invasive – surgery, scans, or examinations?   *surgery*

Reading Test 2

Item 1: A

Item 2: C

Item 3: A and D

Item 4: A and C

Item 5: B, D, C, E, A

Item 6: C, B, E, A, D

Item 7:

(1) project

(2) claiming

(3) overwhelmed

(4) paint

Item 8:

(1) words

(2) correspondence

(3) hypothesis

(4) languages

Item 9:

(1) about

(2) upon

(3) from

(4) in

(5) during

Item 10:

(1) joyful

(2) attainable

(3) idealistic

(4) stressful

Item 11:

(1) C

(2) D

(3) B

(4) A

(5) D

(6) A

Item 12:

(1) B

(2) C

(3) A

(4) D

Item 13:

(1) D

(2) A

(3) C

(4) B

Item 14:

(1) B

(2) C

(3) A

(4) D

Item 15:

(1) A

(2) B

(3) C

(4) A

Listening Test 2

Item 1: The number of teenage smokers began to decline in the late 1990's, although adult smoking had been dropping for years before that time. Research indicates that fifty percent more teenagers smoke than adults. The reasons for this are pressure from peers, the desire of teenagers to conform to the behavior of their social groups, parents' long work schedules, and teenagers' feelings of isolation and alienation.

Item 2: For balanced nutrition, we should consume food from four categories: carbohydrates, fruit, vegetables, and protein. Carbohydrates have been maligned in the media, but they are necessary because they deliver energy to the body. We should also consume a variety of at least five servings of fruit and vegetables every day. Lean protein is best, and we should limit the amount of fatty protein we consume.

Item 3: The correct answers are A, D, and E.

Item 4: The correct answers are A and E.

Item 5: When most of us think of deserts, we recall (1) <u>sandy</u> deserts such as the Sahara, which consists of over ten thousand square miles of sand-covered (2) <u>terrain</u>. Contrary to the popular belief that deserts are vast, sandy (3) <u>wastelands</u>, only about one-fifth of the desert area on earth is covered with sand. The largest desert in the world, the Antarctica desert, covers roughly five and a half (4) <u>million</u> square miles of land space. The Artic desert is second-largest with a size of 5.4 million square miles of land space. Both of these deserts consist (5) <u>predominantly</u> of snow and ice, rather than sand.

Item 6: Organic farming has become one of the fastest growing trends in (1) <u>agriculture</u> recently. Farmers have realized that organic farming is an incredibly cost (2) <u>effective</u> method because it can potentially be used to control costs, as well as to appeal to higher-priced markets. Apart from these (3) <u>monetary</u> benefits, organic farming also naturally results in positive (4) <u>ecological</u> outcomes for the environment. Organic farming relies on practices that do not harm the environment, and for this reason, chemicals and (5) <u>synthetic</u> medicines are prohibited. All kinds of agricultural products can be produced organically, including grains, meat, eggs, and milk. Research has shown that organic produce contains lower levels of both chemicals and (6) <u>bacteria</u> than food which is produced using conventional farming methods. Scientists have discovered that organic farms contain more species of plants, birds, and insects due to the fact that the (7) <u>absence</u> of chemicals from pesticides and fertilizers makes these areas richer habitats for animals.

Item 7: The correct answer is B.

Item 8: The correct answer is D.

Item 9: The correct answer is C.

Item 10: The correct answer is A.

Item 11: The correct answer is B. *Fare* in this context means food.

Item 12: The correct answer is C. *Avert* means to avoid something.

Item 13: *For answers 13 and 14, the incorrect words are underlined and the correct words have been placed in brackets.*

Cell differentiation occurs when a cell changes into another type of cell or cells. Cellular differentiation occurs in multiple [multicellular] organisms. Cells differentiate when they change from a zygote into a more complicated [complex] cellular system. A zygote is a single-celled eukaryotic cell, formed when reproduced [reproductive] cells unite at fertilization. When cells have fully differentiated, they become specialist [specialized]. For this reason, cell differentiation is sometimes referred to as cell specialization. After differentiation, specialized cells experience [undergo] changes in their cytoplasm. Specialized cells also take on unique shapes and the cells can then do one specialized job. These changes in the shapes of specialized cells, as well as the chemical changes, allow [enable] the cells to perform their unique jobs within the organism. In this way, cells are altered [adapted] to perform their special functions to become well suited to the jobs they have to do.

Item 14: Beginning on January 1st, all international students will be required to perform [participate] in a "buddy" system. This system is designed to help international students improve their English language skills, as well as to help them become accustomed [acquainted] with university practices. While grades are not given under this system, participation in the scheme is a necessary requirement for graduating [graduation]. Any student who is able to provide sufficient [satisfactory] evidence of possessing a certificate in English will be excused [exempt] from participating in the scheme. This includes students who have passed a recognized English language professional [proficiency] examination. Students who have received Baccalaureate [Bachelor] of Arts or Science degrees and are now studying for graduate degrees will also not need to participate.

Item 15: For questions about financial aid, you can make an appointment online.

Item 16: The biology exam will take place on the last Thursday of this month.

Item 17: Students must work in groups of three in order to complete the project.

Speaking Test 3 Answers

You should be able to read each item aloud in under 40 seconds for items 1 to 3 and in under 35 seconds for items 4 to 6. The words with primary emphasis are <u>underlined</u> and the words with secondary emphasis are in *italics*. The items without emphasis are in normal font.

Go to "Read Aloud Examples – Test 3" at pte-listening.examsam.com and repeat each item under timed conditions in order to practice your speed, pronunciation, and emphasis.

Item 1: <u>Static electricity</u> *develops* when articles acquire an <u>electrical charge</u> by *rubbing against* one another, such as running a <u>brush</u> through *human hair* or placing a <u>party balloon</u> against clothing. Making contact in this way *transfers* <u>electrons</u> between the two items, causing energy to <u>build up</u>. <u>High volumes</u> of energy can sometimes originate in this way, and <u>dangerous electrical sparks</u> can even be *formed*.

Item 2: <u>South Africa</u> was settled by the <u>Dutch</u> and the <u>British</u> over <u>three hundred</u> years ago. Its economy experienced <u>huge growth</u> as a result of the discovery of the massive <u>gold</u> and <u>diamond</u> *deposits* which are characteristics of its *geology*. The *South African economy* is <u>also</u> bolstered by its <u>grain</u> and <u>citrus</u> fruit crops, as well as the *manufacture* of <u>chemicals</u>, <u>vehicles</u>, <u>machinery</u>, <u>clothing</u>, and <u>electronics</u>.

Item 3: <u>Modern horses</u> are thought to have evolved from two broad *wild* <u>ancestral</u> *types*: the <u>heavy forest</u> *type* and the <u>lighter</u> *flat-land type*. With a <u>muscular</u> *body* and <u>slender</u> *legs*, the <u>quarter</u> *horse* was developed in order to be able to run a *quarter mile* with great <u>strength</u> and <u>endurance</u>. This subspecies is <u>normally</u> around *five feet in height* and is popular with <u>ranchers</u> and others tending to *large groups* of livestock.

Item 4: <u>Virtual reality</u> is a *computing* technique in which a person views an <u>output screen</u>, generally worn as a <u>headset</u>, with all of the participant's <u>movements</u> and <u>sounds</u> *recorded* by the VR system. *Flight* simulators for <u>pilots</u>, <u>video conferencing</u> *platforms*, and <u>computer</u> *games* all rely upon virtual reality systems.

Item 5: The <u>Save</u> *the* <u>Children</u> <u>Fund</u> is the *largest* <u>international</u> children's charity, founded in the *United Kingdom* and having the <u>Princess</u> as its *president*. Working together with <u>other</u> *foundations* around the world, it is concerned with *rescuing children* from *disaster* and the long-term <u>care</u> and <u>welfare</u> of *children* in need.

Item 6: <u>Statistics</u> deals with the <u>collection</u> and <u>analysis</u> of *numerical data*. *Statistical analysis of data* results in the <u>compilation</u> of information that is *useful* to the *general public*, such as the indication of <u>averages</u> for a *given* <u>population</u> and the potential reasons why there are <u>variances</u> from those averages <u>within</u> the population.

Item 7: All candidates for the job will be notified of the outcome by email.

Item 8: Students need to hand in their forms to the Accommodation Office.

Item 9: During the outbreak, many people were infected with the disease.

Item 10: Students often find time management more difficult at the end of the semester.

Item 11: The professor usually arrives a couple of minutes late.

Item 12: There's a good coffee shop near the parking lot on campus.

Item 13: Several books have already been printed on this subject.

Item 14: She should speak with a university representative to clarify the situation.

Item 15: When the immigration rate increases, the population generally expands.

Item 16: The student union will be closed until further notice.

Item 17: The chart reveals how many residents of Cedar Valley have one or more relatives living within a one-mile radius of town. The data indicates that seventy-five people living in the town have one relative within the one-mile radius. The graph shows that the number of residents with more than one family member in proximity to the town declines as the number of relatives within the one-mile zone increases. The lowest figure is that there are only ten residents having five relatives living within one mile of town.

Item 18: The pie chart indicates the amount of kilowatt hours of electricity used by eight different dwellings on Maple Street during the previous week. Two houses came in jointly with the highest consumption at one thousand five hundred hours of kilowatt usage each. The property with the lowest electricity usage had two hundred and one kilowatt hours of consumption, while the other homes ranged from one thousand two hundred and forty-two hours to two hundred and eighty-nine kilowatt hours of electricity.

Item 19: The line graph displays the outdoor exercise preferences relative to rainy weather for three different age groups. We can discern that the desire to exercise outdoors steadily diminishes as the rain increases for those aged sixty-five and over. Yet, there are only modest fluctuations in outdoor exercise activity for the other two age groups when the rainfall goes up. Finally, those who are eighteen years old and younger exercise outdoors far less than the nineteen to sixty-four age group.

Item 20: The graph presents data on predicted class attendance at the next game for four different classes. At over fifty percent attendance, the freshmen class had the highest percentage of students wanting to go to the game, while the sophomore and senior classes had the lowest percentages of those planning on attending. Notably, more than forty percent of the sophomore class was undecided about attending the game, and over forty percent of the senior class had already decided not to be present.

Item 21: The illustration shows the cumulative time in minutes and miles traveled for Aircraft Number two-seventy-five for the previous day. The vessel was airborne for one hundred and twenty minutes and traveled almost eight hundred miles in total during this time. Given that nearly four hundred miles had been traveled at sixty minutes and realizing that the graph increases at a steady rate, we can assume that the aircraft traveled at a more-or-less constant speed during this time.

Item 22: The bar chart highlights in ten-minute increments the amount of time it took Alex Jones to run a particular race. It took him ninety minutes altogether to cover the race course, and the total distance appears to have been around nine or ten miles, since there are nine bars on the chart. He started with his fastest pace, ran more slowly for the next two miles, and then his pace became steady, apart from the forty and ninety-minute intervals.

Item 23 – Text

All fish have two common traits: they live in water and they have bones. Yet, the various species of fish can differ greatly from one another. Sharks are the largest types of fish. And while many fish develop from eggs, sharks actually give birth to their young. Some fish have the typical shape that we expect, but others have bodies more like snakes. There are also other fish that you might have difficulty identifying as a fish. The seahorse has a tiny curled body and has a head like a horse, hence the name seahorse. Now, one reason sea life is so varied is because water covers over seventy percent of our planet, and fish live in a such a variety of places, including lakes, rivers, and the ocean. Another factor is that fish are unique on the evolutionary scale, because, over time, their senses have developed in a special way. They rely less on their vision and more on their hearing, taste, and, smell.

Item 23 – Example Response

The speaker states that all fish have two characteristics in common: the facts that they live in water and have bones. Sharks are the largest fish, and they give birth to their offspring, instead of them growing from eggs. Some fish have the expected shape, but there are others like the seahorse or even snake-like fish. Sea life is varied because water covers seventy percent of the earth. Finally, fish have evolved in a unique way since they rely on hearing, taste, and smell more than sight.

Item 24 – Text

Speaker 1: In today's discussion, we're going to look at child development and educational psychology. The scholastic community still debates principles within these disciplines today, but perhaps the most widely accepted theory deal with the processes by which human beings learn how to exist in their environments. In other words, the basic scope of research covers the question: "How do human beings obtain knowledge?" Dr. Domani, can you talk a bit now about how biology affects child development?

Speaker 2: Yes, I'd be happy to. Thanks. Maybe first of all we should look at the term "abstract symbolic reasoning." This term refers to the idea that biology affects child development much more than environment does. Researchers have discovered that younger children respond to research questions differently than older children, and the conclusion has been reached – which is now more or less universally accepted as fact – that younger children respond to these questions more simply not because they are less intelligent, but because they are at a lower level of biological development.

Item 24 – Example Response

The speakers describe how humans learn how to interact within their environments and obtain knowledge. They explain that biology affects child development more than the environment does, and the term "abstract symbolic reasoning" describes this phenomenon. Research reveals that younger children respond to the same questions more simply than older children do, but this is down to biological development rather than intelligence.

Item 25 – Text

Speaker 1: Today were going to talk with Professor Heinz about Roman history and the fall of the Roman Empire in the fifth century. Professor, can you set the scene in France for us?

Speaker 2: Consider the following scene . . . It is December 406 A.D. in what is now Germany. It is a bitterly cold winter, and the Rhine River is frozen. It was on this site that 15,000 warriors crossed the ice and traveled into the Roman Empire of Gaul.
This invasion, although a seemingly minor incident at the time, later transpired to be one of the most significant episodes in the history of the western world.

Speaker 1: Okay, why was this invasion so significant?

Speaker 2: A new historical epoch would soon be established on this former Roman Empire. Now . . . even though the period has diminished in historical significance in comparison to more recent events, the demise of the Roman Empire was certainly unprecedented in the fifth century.

Speaker 1: I understand. So, part of its significance was that it had never really happened that way before. How do scholars view this time period?

Speaker 2: There were, in fact, many important developments during this time. Specifically, farming communities were established throughout this historical period, meaning that most people were involved in agrarian pursuits. Farmers also developed several farming implements, such as the plow and the water mill. As these agricultural communities thrived, families were better able to support themselves, because, obviously, the food supply was more predictable and abundant. This led to the establishment of a new and vital society on this former Roman Empire.

Item 25 – Example Response

The speaker says that an invasion took place in France in four-o-six when fifteen thousand German warriors crossed over the frozen Rhine River in the winter. The invasion was important because this established the start of a new historical period and new society. As the Roman Empire ended, farming and agriculture developed extensively, and this led to a better food supply and growing communities within the new society.

Item 26: What would you most likely serve with a savory meal - chocolate, gravy, or whipped cream? *gravy*

Item 27: Which item is the most noxious - salad oil, spice, or petroleum? *petroleum*

Item 28: What part of the body does a dermatologist deal with? *the skin*

Item 29: What do people wear if they cannot usually see without them? *eyeglasses or spectacles*

Item 30: In birds, is the purpose of plumage to attract a mate, to hide, or to hunt for food? *to attract a mate*

Item 31: What kind of items would you find in a bouquet - weapons, car parts, or flowers? *flowers*

Item 32: How many parties are there in a unilateral decision? *one*

Item 33: Which phrase best describes an epidemic: a dangerous disease or a mild health problem? *a dangerous disease*

Item 34: Which of the following are used to tie up shoes - braces, stirrups, or laces? *laces*

Item 35: Which one is the largest - a gram or a kilogram? *A kilogram*

Reading Test 3

Item 1: B

Item 2: D

Item 3: C and E

Item 4: A and C

Item 5: C, D, B, E, A

Item 6: B, D, A, E, C

Item 7:

(1) setting

(2) different

(3) educational

(4) advising

Item 8:

(1) primitive

(2) ensuring

(3) level

Item 9:

(1) objective

(2) global

(3) geological

(4) gravitational

Item 10:

(1) finance

(2) stability

(3) automation

(4) downturn

(5) regulations

Item 11:

(1) C

(2) A

(3) B

(4) D

(5) C

(6) B

Item 12:

(1) A

(2) D

(3) C

(4) B

Item 13:

(1) A

(2) C

(3) B

(4) D

Item 14:

(1) D

(2) C

(3) A

(4) B

Item 15:

(1) C

(2) B

(3) A

(4) D

Listening Test 3

Item 1: Teachers understand that students have different ability levels, from below-average to above-average. While some students will always be learning at their optimal levels individually, the teacher needs to be aware of both the struggling students and those who need more difficult challenges. Question adjustment, or asking questions at various levels of difficulty from easy to advanced, is a strategy that teachers can use to reach all students at their differing levels of readiness.

Item 2: Cell division is a normal anatomical process, but when cells in the body experience uncontrolled abnormal divisions, cancer can develop. Tumors can grow from this phenomenon, and sometimes these growths undergo metastasis and spread to other places in the body. While tumors can be removed, they sometimes reappear. Smoking cessation, good dietary choices, and limiting sun exposure can all help to lessen cancer risk.

Item 3: The correct answers are D and E.

Item 4: The correct answers are A and B.

Item 5: As we all know, the genetic characteristics of any (1) <u>organism</u> are present in its DNA. So, DNA is the genetic (2) <u>material</u> found in each and every living cell. These form a genetic code and are formed from long (3) <u>molecules</u> like chains, and these DNA chains consist of four separate (4) <u>components</u> called nucleotides. Okay, that's a bit of a difficult term. I'd better put that one on the board: "nucleotides." It's the order of these nucleotides on the DNA chain that determines the (5) <u>reproductive</u> information for the cells.

Item 6: I can't reveal any information about what's going to be covered on the end-of-(1) <u>semester</u> test. But I can tell you that it is a comprehensive test. When a student has a (2) <u>medical</u> condition, it is considered to be an (3) <u>extenuating</u> circumstance, so we can excuse your absence. We will also have to give you more (4) <u>leeway</u> about your homework and so on. As I said, I really can't give (5) <u>precise</u> details about the final exam, anything we have talked about in class can be included on the final exam. There was a 300-word personal (6) <u>response</u> piece that's due next Tuesday, but if you can give me a note from your doctor as (7) <u>evidence</u>, I can give you a two-week extension. Now, here are copies of the PowerPoint slides. Is there anything else I can help you with?

Item 7: The correct answer is C.

Item 8: The correct answer is A.

Item 9: The correct answer is D.

Item 10: The correct answer is B.

Item 11: The correct answer is D.

Item 12: The correct answer is C.

Item 13: *For answers 13 and 14, the incorrect words are underlined and the correct words have been placed in brackets.*

This lecture provides examples of differentiated cells in palisades [plants] and animals, as well as details about their size [shape] and functions. Palisade cells are found on the top side of the leaves of plants. Full of chloroplasts, which help with the procedure [process] of photosynthesis, root hair cells in plants are long and thick [thin]. They increase the surface area of the top [root] of the plant, helping with the adaptation [absorption] of water and minerals. As far as animal cells, ciliated cells are small hair-like structures that are found in the evaporatory [respiratory] system. They help to filter the air and to move mucus. Nerve cells are made up of long fibers. Charges [Impulses] travel along the fibers to the brain.

Item 14: The tradition of music in the eastern [western] world – in other words, music as we know it today – originated in the genre of chanting. Prior to the thirteenth century, chant was the dominant style [mode] of music. Notably, chanting was a monophonic form of music. Now, "monophonic," let's have a look at that word. "mono" is from a Greek word. It means one thing alone or by itself. "Phonic" is also Greek in originality [origin], and it means sound. So, monophonic music consists of only one sound or vocal [voice] that combines various notes in a series. Polyphonic music appeared in the sixteenth [fifteenth] century, during the early Renaissance period. In contrast to monophonic music, polyphonic music composes [consists] of more than one voice or instrument, and it combines the notes from the different sources together simultaneously. As polyphony developed, musical traditions began to change, and this meant that music began to rely on a greater quality [range] of voices.

Item 15: Your professor is ill today, so class is cancelled for today and tomorrow.

Item 16: All international students must have an interview to get a degree in English.

Item 17: Any student who copies essays from the internet will receive a mark of zero.